Robert Klimmt

Besser in

Englisch

9. Klasse

Gymnasium

Cornelsen
SCRIPTOR

Über den Autor:
Robert Klimmt ist ein erfahrener Englischlehrer.

Bildquellen:
Bibliographisches Institut, Mannheim: S. 56; picture-alliance/ASA, Frankfurt am Main S. 91; picture-alliance/dpa, Frankfurt am Main: S. 62; picture-alliance/epa, Frankfurt am Main: S. 59; Picture-Alliance, ZB, Frankfurt am Main: S. 96

Bibliografische Information der Deutschen Nationalbibliothek
Die Deutsche Nationalbibliothek verzeichnet diese Publikation in der Deutschen Nationalbibliografie; detaillierte bibliografische Daten sind im Internet über http://dnb.d-nb.de abrufbar.

2. Auflage

Bibliographisches Institut GmbH
Dudenstraße 6, 68167 Mannheim

Redaktionelle Leitung: Constanze Schöder
Redaktion: lüra - Klemt & Mues GbR
Herstellung: Annette Scheerer
Layoutkonzept: Horst Bachmann, Weinheim
Umschlaggestaltung: glas AG, Seeheim-Jugenheim
Satz/Layout: Carola Fuchs, Berlin
Druck und Bindung: orthdruk, Białystok
Printed in Poland

ISBN 978-3-411-87080-6

Liebe Schülerin, lieber Schüler,

du hast hier ein Buch zum Lernen, Wiederholen und Üben in der Hand.
- Die Themen sind in kleinen, verständlichen Schritten aufbereitet.
- Schaffe dir parallel zu diesem Buch ein Arbeitsheft an, in das du hineinschreiben kannst.
- Ein Lösungsheft hilft dir, deine Ergebnisse zu kontrollieren.
- Mit der beiliegenden CD und vielen Übungen dazu kannst du dein Hörverstehen trainieren. Folgender Hinweis zeigt dir, wo du die CD verwenden musst: **Track**

Mit diesem Buch kannst du auf zweierlei Weise arbeiten:
1. Möglichkeit:
Wenn du dich im Fach Englisch insgesamt ein wenig unsicher fühlst, solltest du das Buch von vorn bis hinten durcharbeiten. Nimm dir aber nicht zu viel auf einmal vor. Bearbeite lieber kleinere Abschnitte und arbeite dafür regelmäßig, vielleicht sogar täglich.
2. Möglichkeit:
Vielleicht kommst du eigentlich gut zurecht, hast aber einige Lücken? Kläre genau, am besten mithilfe deiner Lehrerin oder deines Lehrers, wo deine Lücken sind. Sieh im Inhaltsverzeichnis nach, wähle einzelne Abschnitte aus und arbeite sie durch.

GOOD TO KNOW **Zum Arbeiten mit diesem Buch**

- Viele Aufgaben kannst du im Buch lösen. Benutze ein **Arbeitsheft,** wenn du viel schreiben musst.
- Bist du beim Lösen der Übungsaufgaben unsicher, schau dir die **Beispiele** dazu noch einmal an.
- Vergleiche deine Ergebnisse immer sorgsam mit dem **Lösungsheft**. Überprüfe genau, was du falsch gemacht hast. Aus Fehlern kann man gut lernen.
- Bearbeite dieselben Aufgaben nach einigen Tagen noch einmal. Die **Wiederholung** schafft Sicherheit.

Viel Spaß und Erfolg beim Lernen!

1 Revision

Du hast schon einiges an englischer Grammatik gelernt.
Mit den Übungen in diesem Wiederholungsteil kannst du herausfinden, ob du mit diesem Band arbeiten kannst. Führe die Übungen durch. Für jede richtige Lösung bekommst du einen oder zwei Punkte. Trage deine Punktzahl unter den Übungen ein und zähle sie dann auf Seite 15 zusammen. Erreichst du weniger als 46 Punkte, solltest du besser noch einmal den Stoff von Klasse 8 wiederholen. Das macht es dir leichter, später die Aufgaben in diesem Buch zu lösen.

REMEMBER *Questions*

Direkte Fragen *(direct questions)* werden mit Hilfsverben (do, can, have, is usw.) gebildet.
Beispiele:
Did Jane show you her new MP3 player?
Can I have some potatoes, please?
Has the maths teacher given you homework today? **Are** you sure?

Frageanhängsel *(question tags)* sind im Englischen üblich. Das sogenannte *tag* (Anhängsel) hat die Form einer Kurzfrage: Hilfsverb + Subjektpronomen.
Beispiele: have I? did she? were they? haven't they? didn't we?

Bei negativen Fragen ist die Form der Kurzfrage positiv, bei positiven Fragen ist sie negativ.
Beispiele:
Jane **hasn't** shown you her new MP3 player yet, **has she?**
You **have** made enough potatoes for all of us, **haven't you?**
The maths teacher **hasn't** given you homework today, **has she?**
You **are** sure, **aren't you?**
He **doesn't** care about the environment, **does he?**

Indirekte Fragen *(indirect questions)* sind Fragen, über die in indirekter Rede berichtet wird. Sie folgen den Regeln für indirekte Rede (passendes Einleitungsverb, *backshift*, Änderung der Zeit- und Ortsangaben) und werden mit if, whether oder einem Fragewort (how, where, what, when usw.) gebildet.
Beispiele:

direkte Frage	**indirekte Frage**
Do you come here often?	He asked me if I often went there.
What school do you go to?	She wanted to know what school I went to.

How does a pressure cooker (Schnellkochtopf) work?	He'd like to know how a pressure cooker works.
Will it rain tomorrow or will it be fine?	He wondered whether it would rain or be fine on the following day.

Indirekte Aufforderungen und Wünsche folgen den Regeln von indirekten Fragen. Passende Verben in diesem Fall sind z. B. ask, tell, want to, expect, invite, remind + Infinitiv mit to.

Beispiele:

direkte Aufforderung/Wunsch	**indirekte Aufforderung/Wunsch**
Don't forget to do the shopping this afternoon.	Dad reminded me to do the shopping that afternoon.
Please don't open that door.	She doesn't want the door to be opened.
You must finish all your homework today.	He expects us to finish all our homework today.
Please keep quiet when I'm playing the piano.	She asked/told us to keep quiet when she was playing the piano.

1 Direct questions: Translate the following questions into English.

1. Bist du schon einmal in London gewesen?
2. Liest du gerade mein Buch?
3. Wolltest du ihm gestern nicht helfen?
4. Hast du letzte Woche mit ihm gesprochen?
5. Wirst du morgen zur Party kommen?

You get 1 point for each correct answer. Your points: ____ /5

2 Question tags: Write the correct tag for the following questions.

1. You haven't seen Katie by any chance, ____________?
2. They weren't living in Leeds at that time, ____________?
3. We saw them last year, though, ____________?
4. You handed your homework in last week, ____________?
5. I haven't given you your pocket money this month yet, ____________?

You get 1 point for each correct answer. Your points: ____ /5

3 Indirect questions: You have just met Jeffrey in London.
Tell a friend about all the questions he asked you.

1. Where have you been?
2. How long will you be in London?

3. What are you doing tomorrow?
4. Did you watch the football match yesterday?
5. Can you give me your mobile number?

You get 1 point for each correct answer. **Your points:** ____ /5

4 Indirect commands, wishes, requests: Tell a friend about them.

1. Can you help me with my homework?
   Henry asked me ____
2. Please don't tell my parents about Sue.
   Henry asked me ____
3. Would you like to come to my birthday party?
   Henry invited me ____
4. Please be there at seven.
   Henry ____
5. Hurry up, we are late.
   Henry ____

You get 1 point for each correct answer. **Your points:** ____ /5

REMEMBER *Negation*

Die folgenden Verben werden einfach mit **not** verneint: be, have und alle Modalverben (can/could, may/might, must, need, will/would, shall/should).
Andere Verben werden im *simple present* mit do not (don't) und im *simple past* mit did not (didn't) verneint. Das folgende Hauptverb ist immer im *bare infinitive* (Infinitiv ohne to).
Denk daran, dass man in negativen Aussagen die any-Wörter benutzt.
Beispiele:

positive Aussage oder Frage	Verneinung
He's in the bedroom.	He is certainly not in the bedroom.
They have already been to London.	No, they haven't been to London yet.
Of course you can see the blackboard.	We can't when you stand in front of it.
You should wear gloves today.	No, I shouldn't – it's not really cold yet.
He lives in London.	No, he doesn't live in London any more.
Most of them enjoyed the play.	Well, I didn't enjoy it at all.
Did you win yesterday?	No, we didn't win. We lost 4:1.
Do you think he'd like a new bicycle?	No, I don't think he would. He really wouldn't like that at all.
John could easily help you with maths.	No, he couldn't help anyone with anything. He needs help himself.

5 **Negate the following statements.**

1. They came to the party.
2. He likes ice-cream.
3. Do it now.
4. You must do your homework today.
5. This machine has always worked.

You get 1 point for each correct answer. Your points: ______ /5

REMEMBER *Use of tenses*

Anders als in anderen westeuropäischen Sprachen besitzen alle Zeiten des englischen Verbs zwei Formen: *simple* und *progressive*. In den *simple*-Formen liegt das Interesse des Sprechers auf der Tatsache, dass etwas vorkommt oder passiert. In den *progressive*-Formen liegt das Interesse auf der laufenden Aktivität oder Handlung. Dieses Interesse nennt man Aspekt (*aspect*): Ausschlaggebend ist immer das Interesse des Sprechers – wie sie oder er die Sache sieht.

Beispiele:	**Erläuterung**
Look at Sarah. She's running really fast. She's just coming up to the last obstacle (Hindernis).	Sarah läuft gerade – die Handlung ist noch nicht abgeschlossen.
Jack runs every day. And he runs beautifully, too. Peter walked down the street and turned left. The house where he was born was still there.	Hier werden Tatsachen als abgeschlossen betrachtet. Es passiert regelmäßig. Alles wird unter dem Aspekt der Abgeschlossenheit bzw. der Tatsachen betrachtet.
Peter was walking down the street. It was raining. He was feeling sad. But then he saw the house where he was born.	Hier stellen drei laufende Handlungen den Hintergrund für eine abgeschlossene Handlung im Vordergrund.

6 **Choose the correct verb forms and tenses.**

Two friends, Jack and Bill, are looking out of the window and chatting about what they see – for example, their neighbour, Mr Anderson. Insert the correct verb forms and tenses in their dialogue.

1. Jack: Can you see what Mr Anderson ______ (do) over there?
2. Bill: Well, I think he ______ (repair) his car. But I ______ (not/be) sure. I ______ (not/can) see him very well.
3. Jack: I ______ (not/think) he is repairing his car. He ______ (repair) his car yesterday. I think he ______ (take) out his shopping.

4. Bill: Oh yes, you're right. But just look at that fence. It looks really nice now he ______ (paint) it.
   Jack: He ______ (start) last Sunday. Every day, he ______ (paint) part of it, and he ______ (finish) the job the day before yesterday. It ______ (be/not) easy. While he ______ (paint) the first part of the fence, it ______ (start) to rain so heavily that he ______ (have to) start again the following day.
5. Bill: Typical. That man ______ (be) always busy with something.
6. Jack: Absolutely. Yesterday he said to my dad: "I ______ (cut down) the old apple tree next week."
7. Bill: How long ______ (Mr Anderson/live) here?
8. Jack: Let me think. As far as I know, he ______ (move) here in 1987, so he ______ (live) here about twenty years now.

You get 1 point for each correct answer. **Your points:** ______ /20

REMEMBER *Conditional clauses*

Ein Bedingungssatz (*conditional clause*) besteht immer aus einem *if*-Satz (*if-clause*) und einem Hauptsatz (*main clause*). Der *if*-Satz beschreibt eine Bedingung und der Hauptsatz drückt aus, was passieren wird oder passieren könnte, wenn diese Bedingung erfüllt wird. Es gibt drei **Grundtypen von Bedingungssätzen:**

- **Typ 1:** Der Sprecher hält die Bedingung für erfüllbar.
- **Typ 2:** Der Sprecher zweifelt an der Erfüllbarkeit der Bedingung.
- **Typ 3:** Der Sprecher weiß, dass die Bedingung nicht mehr erfüllt werden kann.

Conditional Clause Type I

Bei Typ 1 steht die erfüllbare Bedingung im *if*-Satz immer im *simple present*. Die Folge der Bedingung steht im Hauptsatz und wird meist mit dem *will-future* gebildet. Neben dem *will-future* werden im Hauptsatz auch häufig modale Hilfsverben wie z. B. can, must, needn't oder der Imperativ verwendet.

Achtung: Anders als im Deutschen darf im *if*-Satz nie das *will-future* stehen: "if + will is ill!".

Bedingungssätze können mit dem *if*-Satz oder dem Hauptsatz beginnen. Beachte die Kommasetzung!

Beispiele:
If you feel thirsty, just help yourself to a drink.
Just help yourself to a drink if you feel thirsty.

Erfüllbare Bedingung im *if*-Satz: ***simple present***	**Folge im Hauptsatz:** ***will-future***
If we get home late,	we'll all go straight to bed.
If you buy a new bike now,	you will have no money left for Christmas.
If you don't listen to me,	you will regret it.

Conditional Clause Type II

Bei Typ 2 steht die angezweifelte, nur theoretisch erfüllbare Bedingung im *if*-Satz im *simple past*. Die Folge im Hauptsatz wird meist mit dem *conditional* (would + *infinitive*) gebildet.
Typ 2 wird verwendet, wenn die Sprecherin bzw. der Sprecher daran zweifelt, dass die Bedingung erfüllbar ist, oder wenn sie/er genau weiß, dass sie nicht erfüllt werden kann.

Das *simple past* im *if*-Satz drückt hier nicht aus, dass die Handlung in der Vergangenheit stattfand, sondern beschreibt eine für unwahrscheinlich oder unmöglich gehaltene Bedingung.
Beispiel:
If I were you ... → Wenn ich du wäre ... / An deiner Stelle ...

Neben dem *conditional* (would + *infinitive*) kannst du im Hauptsatz auch could/might + *infinitive* verwenden.
Beispiel:
If I had lots of money, I could buy an island. → Wenn ich eine Menge Geld hätte, könnte ich eine Insel kaufen.

Achtung: Anders als im Deutschen darf im *if*-Satz nie das *conditional* stehen.
→ Verwende niemals would, could, might usw. im *if*-Satz: "if + would is no good!".

Beispiele:

angezweifelte Bedingung im *if*-Satz: ***simple past***	***Folge im Hauptsatz: conditional (would + infinitive)***
If I won the lottery,	I would buy you a house.
If I had a new suit,	I'd wear it to the wedding.
If I were you, then,	I'd go out and buy one straight away.

Conditional Clause Type III

Bei Typ 3 steht die nicht mehr erfüllbare Bedingung im *if*-Satz im *past perfect*. Die Folge im Hauptsatz muss *conditional perfect* (would + have + *past participle*) sein.

Typ 3 wird verwendet, wenn die Sprecherin bzw. der Sprecher weiß, dass die Bedingung nicht mehr erfüllt werden kann, weil es sich um eine abgeschlossene Situation handelt, die in der Vergangenheit stattgefunden hat.

Beispiel:

If you had not broken your bike, your parents would not have bought you a new one.
→ Wenn du dein Fahrrad nicht kaputt gemacht hättest, hätten dir deine Eltern kein neues gekauft.

Auch im Typ 3 kann man neben would auch could oder might benutzen.

Beispiele:

nicht mehr erfüllbare Bedingung im *if*-Satz: *past perfect*	**Folge im Hauptsatz: *conditional perfect* (would + have + *past participle*)**
If he had known how dangerous it is,	he would not have gone surfing there.
If you had helped me with maths,	I would have passed the test.
If I'd had the money,	I would certainly have bought that bike.

7 Choose the right verb forms in the following conditional sentences.

1. Come on, let's hurry. My aunt will be quite annoyed if we ______________ (not get) there on time.
2. We will have a barbecue if the weather ____________ (to be) fine.
3. If you ______________ (take) the 7.30 train, you will arrive at 9.15.
4. If I found a purse in the street, I __________________ (take) it to the nearest police station.
5. We would move to London if my parents ________________ (can get) jobs there.
6. If he _________________ (win) the lottery, he would buy a big sports car.
7. If my dad had not lost his job, he ____________________ (be) nicer to us when we were kids.
8. I ________________ (work) harder if they had paid me better.
9. If I had known his address, I _______________ (visited) him.

You get 1 point for each correct answer. Your points: ____ /9

8 Mixed bag.

Complete the following sentences. Use your own ideas.

1. If they hadn't been late, ______________________
2. You will soon feel better if ______________________
3. I wouldn't mind you borrowing my umbrella if ______________________
4. We wouldn't have been able to get home if you ______________________

You get 1 point for each correct answer. Your points: ____ /4

REMEMBER *Modal verbs*

Die wichtigsten Modalverben des Englischen sind can/could, may/might, will/would, shall/should, must und needn't.
Die folgende Tabelle bietet eine Übersicht:

Modalverb	Beispiel	Bedeutung	Funktion
can	Can I come in?	Darf ich ...	Bitte
	She can jump 2.5 metres.	Sie kann ...	Fähigkeit
	You can come tomorrow.	Du darfst/kannst ...	Erlaubnis
could	Could you open the window?	Könntest du ...	höfliche Bitte
	I could come tomorrow.	Ich könnte ...	Möglichkeit
may	May I have a piece of cake?	Darf ich ...	höfliche Bitte
	He may come tomorrow.	Er könnte ...	Möglichkeit
might	He might come tomorrow.	Er könnte vielleicht ...	Möglichkeit (schwach)
must	He must be upstairs.	Er muss/müsste ...	Wahrscheinlichkeit
	You must get up now.	Du musst ...	Verpflichtung (stark)
mustn't	You mustn't hit him like that.	Du darfst ihn nicht ...	Verbot
needn't	You needn't get up just yet.	Du musst nicht ...	keine Verpflichtung
	She needn't give it back.	Sie muss es nicht ...	
will	She simply won't understand.	Sie wird nicht ...	Vermutung
would	He would do that sort of thing.	Das sieht ihm ähnlich.	Rüge
shall	We shall overcome.	Wir werden siegen.	Entschlossenheit
should	You should tell him about it.	Du solltest ihm ...	dringender Rat

Modalverb	Beispiel	Bedeutung	Funktion
should	They should be here soon.	Sie sollten bald ...	Wahrscheinlichkeit
	We should go and see her.	Wir sollten ...	Verpflichtung (schwach)
	I should have done it earlier.	Ich hätte es ... sollen.	

9 **Translate the following sentences into English.**

1. Wir müssen jetzt noch nicht anfangen.
2. Mir ist schlecht. Ich hätte diese drei Hamburger nicht essen sollen.
3. Es wäre vielleicht besser gewesen, wenn wir zu Hause geblieben wären.
4. Ich darf nicht vergessen, ihn zu fragen.
5. Gestern durften wir bis 23.00 Uhr fernsehen.

You get 2 points for each correct sentence. Your points: ______ /10

REMEMBER *The passive*

Das Passiv wird mit einer Form des Hilfsverbs be und dem *past participle* (3. Form) gebildet.

Beispiele:

Dinner is always served at 7 in the evening.
The book was sent by post.
The painting was stolen last night.
I have been asked to speak to you about your son.
The students have been informed about the new lunch times.
She had been told that the electric current was switched off.

10 **Insert the correct passive forms of the verb in the following sentences.**

1. Just ten minutes after the accident, the woman ______ (take) to hospital.
2. Manchester could not play yesterday. The match ______ (cancel).
3. My computer ______ (repair). It is working all right now.
4. Oh dear, my bike has gone. It ______ (must/steal).
5. The new building ______ (open) last week.

You get 1 point for each correct answer. Your points: ______ /5

REMEMBER *Adjectives and adverbs*

Adjektive und Adverbien machen Aussagen genauer und abwechslungsreicher.

- **Adjektive** beschreiben ein Nomen. Sie stehen in der Regel nach dem Verb to be oder vor einem Substantiv.
  Beispiele:
  She is tall.
  He is a strong swimmer.

- **Adverbien** beziehen sich meistens auf ein Verb. Sie können sich aber auch auf Adjektive oder andere Adverbien beziehen. Sie stehen nach dem Vollverb, dem ersten Hilfsverb oder einem Objekt.
  Beispiele:
  He ate the pizza hungrily.
  He ran the race extremely fast.
  She is an outstandingly good scientist.
  I had scarcely entered the room when the telephone rang.

- **Adverbiale Bestimmungen (*adverbials*)** sind Wortgefüge, die die Funktion eines Adverbs erfüllen.
  Beispiele:
  Let's meet at the station.
  He was walking down the road in a great hurry.

11 Translate the following sentences into English.

1. Er ist extrem gut für diese Arbeit qualifiziert.
2. Das schmeckt gut.
3. Sie arbeiten hart.
4. Sie sieht nett aus.
5. Er sang schön.
6. Sie kann schnell laufen.
7. Wir fahren einmal im Jahr nach Berlin.
8. Er trägt immer eine Baseballkappe.
9. Wir fliegen um 4.00 Uhr morgens nach London.

You get 2 points for each correct sentence. Your points: ____ /18

Your total points out of 92 points: ____

If you have less than 46 points you should look at the book for year 8 again. That will make it easier for you to do the exercises in this book.

2 Sprache verstehen

Das solltest du am Ende der Klasse 9 können:

- ▷ Die Zeiten kennen und richtig verwenden
- ▷ Den Unterschied zwischen Sätzen mit Gerundium und Sätzen mit Infinitiv kennen und das Gerundium verwenden
- ▷ Relativ- sowie Konditionalsätze bilden
- ▷ Das Passiv sicher einsetzen
- ▷ Sätze in indirekter Rede bilden
- ▷ Präpositionen kennen und im Satzzusammenhang verwenden
- ▷ Gesagtes oder Textinhalte vom Deutschen ins Englische übertragen und umgekehrt

Otto in an English restaurant:
"Waiter, I become a beefsteak, and my friend here becomes a desert."
Das ist ein typischer Fehler, den Deutsche im Englischen machen: Otto hat „bekommen" mit „become" verwechselt, da sie ähnlich klingen.
Man sollte nicht vergessen: Alle machen Fehler, auch Muttersprachler. Für den Sprachlernenden sind Fehler daher eigentlich nichts Schlimmes, sie gehören zum Lernprozess und werden von Muttersprachlern fast immer verziehen. Sie verhindern nicht unbedingt die Kommunikation, solange noch zu erraten ist, was gemeint ist.

2.1 *Modality and politeness*

REMEMBER *Knowing the difference*

Modalverben dienen der Qualifizierung eines Vollverbs. So drücken Modalverben wie can, may, must, could, should aus, ob jemand etwas tun kann oder könnte (can, could), darf (may), sollte (should), oder sogar muss (must).
Die Modalverben stehen vor dem Infinitiv des Vollverbs. (I can go home.)
Wie im Deutschen ist es auch im Englischen wichtig, die Bedeutungsunterschiede der einzelnen Modalverben zu kennen und sie situationsgerecht anzuwenden. Ansonsten kann es zu Missverständnissen kommen und du kannst schnell als unhöflich (*impolite*) oder sogar als grob und unverschämt (*rude*) angesehen werden.

Trouble spot: must
Das englische Wort must hat einen wesentlich härteren Klang als das deutsche *muss*. Formulierungen mit must werden von Muttersprachlern eventuell als unhöflich und bevormundend gesehen.

Beispiele:

You must be careful with the dish washer. Gemeint ist: → Please be careful with ...

We must do the washing up. Höflicher wäre es so: → Mum and Dad would like us to do the washing up.

Wenn du die Bedeutung *müssen* ausdrücken willst, verwende lieber eine **Alternative**, ob Modal- oder Vollverb: z. B. should, ought to, have to, need to.

Beispiele:

You must understand him. → You have to/should try to

Must you come into my room every day? → I'd rather you didn't ...

You must work harder. → I think you ought to/should ...

You must think about it more carefully. → You need to ... / You should ...

In diesen Fällen kannst du must benutzen:

- Vermutung bzw. Gewissheit ausdrücken:
  You have had a really long flight. You must be tired.
  Where is my car key? I must have it somewhere.
- Eine starke Empfehlung ausdrücken:
  You must see this film. It's brilliant. An absolute must.
- Eine (starke) Verpflichtung ausdrücken:
  You must get up now.
  Homework must be handed in by the end of the week.

Andere Alternativen zu must not:

You **are not supposed to** use these bikes without permission.
We **are not allowed to** stay out till midnight during the week.
We **shouldn't really** go to that place. It's not safe.
Please don't smoke in here.
Would you mind not smoking in here?
Please refrain from smoking in here.

1 Using polite forms

Your mother wants to talk to the exchange student who is staying with you for the next two weeks. As she doesn't know any English, she asks you to put the following instructions into English. You don't need to translate her sentences word by word, but you should make sure that what you say sounds polite.

1. In unserem Haus muss jeder mit anpacken.
2. Du musst jeden Tag den Müll rausbringen.
3. Du musst bis zehn zu Hause sein.

2.2 *Tenses*

REMEMBER *Expressing the future*

Will-future **und** ***going to-future***

Es gibt Bedeutungsunterschiede zwischen *will-future* und *going to-future*. Hier ist eine kurze Übersicht:

going to-future	*will-future*
Absicht / schon entschiedener Plan:	**Spontane Entscheidung:**
"Bill and I have decided to go to Anne's place. Allen's dad is going to take us there. Do you want to come along?" (Allens Vater hat bereits im Voraus erklärt, dass er sie mitnimmt – der Fokus liegt hier auf seiner Absicht.)	Bill: "Anne has just called." Bob: "Great, I'll call her back in a minute." (Bob reagiert spontan auf die Situation und trifft dabei erst die Entscheidung.)
Zwingend eintreffende Handlung:	**Allgemeine Voraussage:**
Look at the sky. It's going to rain. I feel awful. I'm going to be sick.	I think there will be more rain next week. They are OK. They won't make any trouble.

1 **Use going to-future or will-future.**

1. A. What would you like to have?
   B. I ________ have a cheeseburger, please.
2. A. Why have you turned on the computer?
   B. I ________ to write an e-mail.
3. A. That bike of yours doesn't look very safe.
   B. I know, I ________ get it fixed this afternoon.
4. A. Oh dear. I have left my money at home.
   B. Don't worry. I ________ lend you some.
5. A. Has your brother decided what to do when he comes home?
   B. Yes, he ________ decorate his room. He has already bought all the paint. By the way, he needs somebody to give him a hand.
   A. No problem. I ________ help him.
6. A. Look, the bus has already left.
   B. Oh no, we ________ be late for school.
7. A. Look, our petrol tank is almost empty and there's no petrol station for the next 50 miles.

B. Oh no. We ______ run out of petrol. What ______ do now?

8. A. Look at those clouds.
   B. There ______ be a thunderstorm any minute.

REMEMBER *Present tenses with future meaning*

Man kann zukünftige Ereignisse auch durch Benutzung der Gegenwart in Form der einfachen Gegenwart (*simple present*) oder der Verlaufsform (*present progressive*) ausdrücken.

Das ***simple present*** als Ausdruck der Zukunft wird benutzt bei Ankündigungen auf Stunden- oder Zeitplänen, wenn also etwas **offiziell** festgelegt ist.
Beispiele:
The film begins at 9 o'clock.
What time does your train leave?
We start school tomorrow.

Das ***present progressive*** als Ausdruck der Zukunft wird vor allem bei persönlichen **Verabredungen** benutzt, d. h. wenn etwas bereits entschieden und arrangiert ist.
Beispiele:
Are you doing anything this evening? → Hast du schon etwas geplant?
Yes, I'm going out with my friends.
Are you playing football tomorrow? No, I'm going to the shops with my Dad.

Das ***present progressive*** wird auch für die Ankündigung einer Handlung benutzt, die sofort in die Tat umgesetzt wird.
Beispiele:
It's past midnight. I'm going to bed now. (Nicht: I go oder I'll go to bed now.)
John: Can you give me a hand?
Ann: Sure, I'm coming. (Sie kommt sofort.)

2 Use the simple present or present progressive to express future activities.
Translate the following sentences into English.
(Tipp: Entscheide erst, ob es sich um eine persönliche Verabredung oder einen offiziellen Termin handelt.)

1. Ich gehe heute Abend ins Kino.
2. Das Konzert beginnt um 20.00 Uhr.
3. Wann fährt der Bus?
4. Lass uns gehen. Kommst du?
5. Was machst du diesen Freitag?
6. Der neue Mathekurs fängt nächste Woche an.

3 Use different ways of expressing the future.

1. Ann: Have you decided what to do next summer?
   John: Sure. I ______ (visit) my uncle in America with my family.
2. Ann: What ______ (you/do) on Friday night?
   John: Me and my friends ______ (go) to a concert. ______ (you/come along)?
3. Ann: I'd like to, but I can't. I have to stay at home and babysit my little brother.
   John: Well, you know what: I ______ (ask) my sister. I think she ______ (do) the babysitting for you, if you promise to help her with her English exams.
   Ann: Sounds like a fair deal. The exams ______ (be) on Thursday so there ______ (be) enough time to get her prepared.
4. Ann: How ______ (get) to the concert?
   John: No problem. There is a bus. It ______ (leave) at eight and ______ (take) us back at twelve thirty.

REMEMBER *Simple present or present progressive?*

Alle Zeiten des englischen Verbs haben **zwei Formen**: *simple* und *progressive*. Beim *simple present* wird eine Tatsache betont, beim *present progressive* liegt das Interesse des Sprechers auf der laufenden Handlung selbst.

Die **Verwendung** der einfachen Gegenwart (*simple present*) und der Verlaufsform (*present progressive*) ist unterschiedlich (s. auch S. 9):

Das ***simple present*** wird für allgemeine Zustände benutzt oder für Sachen, die immer wieder passieren, z. B. eine Gewohnheit oder eine Situation, die regelmäßig eintritt.
Beispiele:
Water freezes at zero degrees.
Excuse me, do you live here?
I play football every afternoon.
I live and work in Germany.
Signalwörter: every day/year, regularly, always, usually, normally, often, twice a week.

Das ***present progressive*** beschreibt Dinge, die gerade in diesem Augenblick (*here and now*) ablaufen und noch nicht beendet sind. Im Deutschen wird dafür oft das Wort „gerade" eingesetzt.

Beispiele:
Look, Johnny **is walking** down the street. → Johnny läuft **gerade** die Straße hinunter.
Can you hear him? He **is talking** to my parents.
Where do you live? Well, at the moment **I'm living** with my uncle.
You **are doing** a good job today. Keep up the good work.
In the present situation many people **are losing** their jobs.
Signalwörter: look!, at the moment, today, in the present situation.

Die unten aufgeführten Verben (sogenannte ***state verbs***) werden in der Regel nicht in der Verlaufsform benutzt, weil sie keine Aktivität sondern einen (häufig inneren) **Zustand** beschreiben. Dieser Zustand ändert sich nicht: Entweder liebe ich oder liebe ich nicht, verstehe ich oder verstehe ich nicht, höre ich oder höre ich nicht – ich kann das nicht ändern:

- Gefühlsverben: love, hate, like, want, need
- Wahrnehmungsverben: hear, see, smell, taste, sound
- Wissensverben: know, understand, realize, suppose, mean, remember
- Zustandsverben: be, belong, own, contain, include

Das Verb to be wird nur in der Verlaufsform (am/is/are being) benutzt, wenn das augenblickliche Verhalten betont wird:
Beispiele:
He **is** normally such a nice person. But right now, he **is being** really strange.
→ Normalerweise ist er nett, nur gerade jetzt verhält er sich äußerst seltsam.
She's being really difficult about it. → Sie macht es wirklich schwierig.

4 Present simple or present progressive? Put in the correct form of the verb.

EXAMPLE

Listen to the the two boys. They ______ (try/sing) but it ______ (sound) awful.
They are trying to sing but it sounds awful.

1. I can see that you are thirsty. ______ (you/want) anything to drink?
2. Susan has walked out on me. I think she ______ (not/love) me anymore.
3. Who is that girl? Why ______ (she/stare) at us? ______ (I/not/know)
4. Come on, please stop. You know how to behave. You ______ (be) really silly about it.
5. Sorry, you can't use my bike today. I ______ (need) it.
6. He told me the name of the place, but I ______ (not/remember) remember it right now.

REMEMBER *Simple past or past progressive?*

Die Verlaufsform der Vergangenheit (*past progressive*) beschreibt eine Aktivität oder Handlung, die gerade ablief, als etwas anderes passierte.

Beispiele:

We were watching TV when Mr K. knocked at the door. → Wir sahen gerade fern, als Herr K. anklopfte.

Jack was driving down the road. The sun was shining and the birds were singing. Suddenly the engine made a strange noise ...

Die Verlaufsform drückt eine **Rahmenhandlung** aus (watching TV/driving usw.), innerhalb derer die eigentliche Handlung stattfindet, um die es dem Erzähler geht (Mr K. knocked at the door/the engine made a strange noise).

5 Put in the correct form of the verb.

While the old lady ______ (do) the washing up, she
suddenly ______ (hear) a strange sound.
She ______ (listen) closely.
There it ______ (be) again.
It ______ (come) from the attic.
She ______ (feel) very scared.
She ______ (pick up) the phone
and ______ (dial) 999. When the police finally
______ (enter) the house, they
______ (see) the old lady in her armchair.
She ______ (snore) peacefully and her cat
______ (play) with a little ball.

REMEMBER *Present perfect: simple and progressive*

Das *present perfect* ***simple*** wird verwendet,

- wenn Handlungen in der Vergangenheit begonnen haben, aber noch nicht abgeschlossen sind:

  Beispiele:

  I have started to clean the room. → ... aber ich bin noch nicht fertig.

  I have lived here for ten years. → ... und lebe immer noch hier.

- wenn Handlungen in der Vergangenheit eine Auswirkung auf die Gegenwart haben oder wenn ein Resultat vorliegt:

Beispiele:
I have cleaned the room. → Bitte sehr, der Raum ist sauber.
I've seen that film already. → ... und will ihn deshalb nicht nochmals sehen.

- um how many/much, how many times auszudrücken:
  Beispiele:
  Bill has eaten three pizzas, so he can't still be hungry.
  I've finished the first chapter already.
  Brazil has won the football World Cup four times.

Das ***present perfect progressive***, also die Verlaufsform des *present perfect*, wird benutzt, wenn

- betont werden soll, dass ein Vorgang **noch im Gange ist.**
  Vergleiche diese Beispiele:
  I have been repairing your bike for hours, but it still doesn't work. → Die Arbeit ist noch nicht abgeschlossen.
  I have repaired your bike. It's in proper working order now. → Es ist fertig.
- die **Dauer** einer Handlung betont werden soll. → how long?
  I have been waiting here for two hours and he still hasn't come.
- eine gerade abgeschlosse **Aktivität** als Begründung für einen Zustand betont werden soll.
  Beispiele:
  Oh, you're really wet. Have you been swimming?
  Your hands are dirty. What on earth have you been doing? – Oh, I've been mending the car.
  → Der gerade abgeschlossene Vorgang (schwimmen/Auto reparieren) **erklärt** den nassen bzw. schmutzigen Zustand der angesprochenen Person.

6 **Put in the right form of the present perfect. Simple or progressive?**

1. Look over there, someone ______ (take) your bike.
2. Look, how sweaty he is. He ______ (cycling) for hours.
3. This is Tom, an exchange student from Scotland. He ______ (live) with our family for 6 months now.
4. Mr King, how long ______ (you/write) horror novels?
5. Mr King, how many novels ______? (you/write)
6. I'm having a party at my place tomorrow. But I can't remember how many people I ______ (invite).
7. Please switch off the box. You ______ (watch) TV for almost 5 hours now.
8. This is Conrad. He ______ (make) films since he was twelve. Actually, he ______ (make) 23 films up to now.

REMEMBER *Present perfect or simple past?*

Das ***simple past*** beschreibt eine **abgeschlossene** Handlung.
Signalwörter: yesterday, last year, a week ago, then, when?
Das Fragewort when fragt immer nach einem abgeschlossenen Zeitpunkt.
Beispiel:
When did you start to learn English?

Das ***present perfect*** bezieht sich auf Dinge, die zwar in der Vergangenheit beginnen, aber **für die Gegenwart noch eine Bedeutung haben**, weil sie entweder noch andauern oder das Ergebnis jetzt relevant ist.
Signalwörter: since 1987, for many years, this week, today, this morning (falls es noch am Morgen ist), ever/never.
Beispiel:
I have lived in London for six years.

7 Check the verb forms of the following sentences. Correct them where necessary.

EXAMPLE

I lost my umbrella. I can't find it anywhere.
wrong: I have lost my umbrella.

1. Dad, have you played a lot of football when you were young?
2. Have you been to England since 1999?
3. Where have you been yesterday?
4. We are looking for Martin. Did you see him?
5. Her father died before she was born.
6. When has he found out that his boss has had an affair with his wife?
7. I have just bought a new CD. Come and listen to it.

REMEMBER *Past perfect: simple and progressive*

Wie der deutsche Name „Vorvergangenheit" sagt, drückt das ***past perfect*** Handlungen aus, die noch vor einem anderen Punkt in der Vergangenheit stattgefunden haben.
Beispiele:
I went up to his house. But he wasn't there. → Ereignis in der Vergangenheit
He had gone out. → Er war schon vorher weg, also **Vor**vergangenheit

Die Verlaufsform des *past perfect,* das *past perfect* ***progressive***, wird benutzt, wenn der Aspekt der andauernden Aktivität bzw. Handlung betont wird.
Beispiele:
They were good friends. They had been playing for the same team for years.
She had been waiting all afternoon for the phone to ring. Now, at last, it had done so. She picked it up nervously ...

8 **Put the verb into the correct form. Use either past perfect or past (simple or progressive).**

EXAMPLE

Did you see Karen at the concert. No, ______ (she already/go) home.
No, she had already gone home.

1. I felt really exhausted when I got home. That's why I ______ (go) straight to bed.
2. Jonathan didn't play very well last Sunday. No wonder, he ______ (never/play) before.
3. Sorry for being late. But the bus ______ (break down) on my way here.
4. Lisa didn't do well in the test. The reason was that she ______ (play) cards the night before, so she didn't get enough sleep.
5. The murderer just managed to escape. Detective Marlowe was furious, as he ______ (follow) him for two years.
6. My parents couldn't sleep last night because their next door neighbour ______ (have) a big party.
7. There was trouble at the entrance of the concert hall because the organizers ______ (not/planned) for so many fans.
8. When I got there, David ______ (be) angry with me because he ______ (wait) for two hours.

REMEMBER *Participles*

Es gibt zwei verschiedene Partizipien:

- das ***present participle*** mit aktiver Bedeutung
  Beispiele:
  I saw him **running** down the street. → Ich sah, wie er die Straße hinunter lief.
  Not **being** in possession of a valid passport he got into real trouble at the border.
  → Da er nicht in Besitz eines gültigen Passes war, ...

▶ das ***past participle*** mit <u>passiver Bedeutung</u>

Beispiele:

They never found the jewels **stolen** during the break-in.

→ Sie fanden die bei dem Einbruch gestohlenen Juwelen nie.

We enjoyed the soup **made** by my father.

→ Wir genossen die von meinem Vater gemachte Suppe.

Wenn eine Aktion vor der anderen stattfindet, dann benutzt man die **Verlaufsform** des *past participle*:

Beispiele:

Having said that he drew a gun and fired at him. → Nachdem er das gesagt hatte, ...

Having eaten three pizzas, he felt rather full.

Partizipialkontruktionen werden eher im Schriftlichen als im Mündlichen verwendet. Sie verkürzen die Sätze und machen sie daher eleganter.

9 Connect the following sentences using a participle construction.

EXAMPLE

They were skiing down a steep slope. Angus hurt his knee.

Angus hurt his knee skiing down a steep slope.

1. I had seen the film three times already. I really didn't want to see it again.
2. He didn't know what to do. He closed the door and pretended he wasn't there.
3. They found him. He was lying on the ground. He had been seriously injured. (two participles)
4. He was caught in the act. So he finally had to admit that he did it.
5. She owns an amazing guitar. It was once played by Jimi Hendrix.
6. The mountains were a fantastic sight. They were covered in snow.

10 Translate the following sentences into German.

1. I don't like being treated like that.
2. Tucked up in bed, he started dreaming of a wonderful day.
3. Sold more than 5 million times, this hit single made him a rich man.
4. I saw her wearing this fantastic dress again.
5. Dave heard someone knocking at the door.

2.3 *Gerund and infinitive*

REMEMBER

Ein Gerundium ist ein Verb, das als **Substantiv** gebraucht wird. Im Englischen wird dafür an den Infinitiv ein *-ing* gehängt.

Beispiele:

Sleep**ing** in hotel beds is not always a pleasure. → Das Schlafen in Hotelbetten ist nicht immer ein Vergnügen.

She loves ski**ing**. → Sie liebt das Skifahren.

I don't like his cook**ing**: he uses too much salt. → Ich mag seine Art zu Kochen nicht, er benutzt zu viel Salz.

He denies murder**ing** the old lady. → Er bestreitet, die alte Dame ermordet zu haben.

I am used to driv**ing** in heavy traffic. → Ich bin daran gewöhnt, bei starkem Verkehr zu fahren.

Wenn die Aktion beendet ist, kann man having + *past participle* verwenden.

Beispiele:

He denied **having murdered** the old lady. → Er bestritt, die alte Dame ermordet zu haben.

Manche Verben werden **immer mit dem Gerundium** verwendet, z. B.:

admit	enjoy	mind
avoid	finish	practise
deny	give up	risk
dislike	go/keep on	suggest

Beispiele:

She dislikes being woken up at that time.

I don't mind giving it a try.

She enjoys writing e-mails to her friends.

He avoided going to cricket practice whenever he could.

Nicht alle Verben werden mit einem Gerundium verbunden: Viele werden mit dem **Infinitiv** mit **to** verwendet, z. B.:

afford	decide	learn	recommend
allow	fail	need	refuse
agree	forget	manage	remember
arrange	hope	promise	threaten

Beispiele:

I forgot to tell him.

She decided not to go.

We can't afford to go on holiday again.

Bei einigen Verben gibt es **Bedeutungsunterschiede,** je nachdem, ob der Infinitiv oder das Gerundium gebraucht wird.

Beispiele:

remember to do something	→ nicht vergessen, etwas zu tun
remember doing something	→ sich erinnern, etwas getan zu haben
forget to do something	→ vergessen, etwas zu tun
forget doing something	→ vergessen, etwas getan zu haben
stop to do something	→ anhalten, um etwas zu tun
stop doing something	→ aufhören, etwas zu tun

Auch einige **Adjektive** sowie mit Adjektiven gebildete Ausdrücke werden mit einem Gerundium verwendet, z. B.:

involved in	worth	keen on	pointless
happy about	interested in	no good (at)	

Beispiele:

It's no good waking her up at that time.
It's worth giving it a try.
It's pointless trying to play in this weather.
He is involved in organising a concert for his friends.
I don't feel like going to cricket practice today.
I'm interested in playing basketball.
I'm keen on staying here with my friends.

1 Gerund or infinitive? Put in the right form of the verb.

EXAMPLE

I am very bad ______ (write) letters.
I am very bad at writing letters.

1. He failed ______ (turn up) on time.
2. I like ______ (be) treated like a king.
3. We hope you don't mind ______ (finish) a bit later.
4. Finally they decided ______ (go out) to the cinema.
5. Where did you learn ______ (drive) a car like that?
6. Our teacher promised ______ (not give) us a test tomorrow.
7. My dad hates ______ (fly).
8. We really enjoyed ______ (travel) to Egypt last year.
9. I am good at ______ (write) compositions.
10. He wasn't interested in ______ (find out) about it.

11. We look forward to ______ (see) you tomorrow.
12. She and I agreed ______ (talk) things over.
13. This museum is worth ______ (visit).
14. We should give up ______ (look) for him.
15. Did he really manage ______ (pass) the exam?

2 Gerund or infinitive with *to*: Translate the following sentences into German.

1. a. Please remember to do the shopping.
   b. I remember doing the shopping that day.
2. a. He stopped to smoke a cigarette.
   b. He stopped smoking cigarettes.
3. a. Did he really forget to tell you about the party?
   b. He will never forget seeing her for the first time.

2.4 *Position of adverbs*

REMEMBER

Adverbien stehen nicht direkt zwischen Verb und Objekt, sondern in der Regel am Ende des Satzes.

Beispiele:

I met my friends **yesterday.**

→ Ich habe gestern meine Freunde getroffen.

She sang the song **well.**

She looked at him **curiously.**

They shouted at him **loudly.**

Verb + Objekt bleiben zusammen: Das Adverb kommt meistens ans Ende. Adverbien, die die **Art und Weise** einer Handlung bestimmen, können aber auch **unmittelbar nach dem Verb** stehen, das diese Handlung ausdrückt.

Beispiele:

They **shouted loudly** at him.

The children **looked curiously** out of the window.

The sun **sank rapidly** behind the clouds.

It **snowed heavily** last January.

Die Reihenfolge bei mehreren Adverbien ist: **Ort vor Zeit vor Art und Weise**.

Beispiele:

John walks **to school** **every morning.**

My mother drives me **to school** **every morning** **in our new car.**

Sometimes, always, ever, never, even in Verbindung mit einem **Vollverb** stehen in der Regel **vor** dem Verb. Bei Vollverb + **Hilfsverb** (z. B. Modalverb) steht das Adverb unmittelbar **vor dem Vollverb**.

Beispiele:

He **always** drives a big Jaguar.
I **sometimes** went over there in the evening.
I **never** go to bed before midnight.
I can **always** depend on him.
He **even** told me to go to hell.
I have **never** liked her.
He might not **even** be there.

Achtung: **Längere adverbiale Bestimmungen** (a long time ago, with great speed) kommen immer ans Ende.
Die **Zeitangabe** kann auch an den **Satzanfang** gestellt werden.

Beispiel:

Every morning, my mother drives me to school in our new car.

1 Correct or incorrect? Cross out the wrong sentences and write down the correct version where necessary.

EXAMPLE

~~He goes always at the weekend to see his mother.~~
→ *He always goes to see his mother at the weekend.*
We will beat them easily. → *correct*

1. He did quickly his homework.
2. She lost also her dinner money.
3. Do you play every day the guitar?
4. Did you talk about it last night?
5. Don't so late go to bed.
6. I can remember her name never.
7. He will probably leave on Friday.
8. She has usually a lot of homework to do.
9. They will be never my friends.
10. We should have never eaten this.
11. Aren't you often lonely?
12. I go every morning to my friend's house.

REMEMBER *To + infinitive, for + noun, for + -ing*

To + infinitive

Damit wird der Zweck einer **Handlung** oder die Folge einer **Eigenschaft** ausgedrückt (entspricht dem Deutschen „um ... zu").

Beispiele:

This fence was built to keep away the wolves.
I don't have time to revise for the test.
He waited to see what she would do.
He was too slow to win the race.
Peter was too lazy to get out of bed.
She went to London to learn English.

For + noun

Auch hier geht es um den Zweck einer Handlung oder die Folge einer **Eigenschaft**. Allerdings ist das Objekt nun ein **Nomen**.

Beispiele:

What would you like for breakfast?
Let's go for a swim.
I can't come. I'm cramming for a test.
I'd love to go for a holiday to Malta.
He was late for the lesson.

For + -ing

For + -ing wird nur benutzt, wenn man die **Funktion** oder den **Zweck** eines **Gegenstandes** beschreibt.

Beispiele:

This machine is used for cutting up potatoes. (or: ... to cut up the potatoes)
We need new shelves for storing all our tools. (or: ... to store)
Those plums are not for eating – I need them for making jam.

2 Translate the following sentences into English.

1. Ich will, dass du mit dem Rauchen aufhörst.
2. Er braucht Geld, um sich eine Fahrkarte zu kaufen.
3. Sie ging ins Krankenhaus, um sich operieren zu lassen.
4. Hat er genug Leibwächter, die ihn beschützen?
5. Ist dies ein spezielles Gerät (= device), um das Auto sauber zu machen?
6. Es tut mir leid zu hören, dass er die Schule verlassen hat.

2.5 *Defining and non-defining relative clauses*

REMEMBER

Der bestimmende Relativsatz enthält die entscheidenden – „definitiven“ bzw. bestimmenden – Informationen über das Subjekt. Diese Relativsätze verwenden **keine Kommas.**

Beispiele:

The boy who came first in the 100 m race also won the field and track competition.
The book that we are using today is lying on my table.

▶ Die Information who came first in the 100 m race bzw. that we are using today ermöglicht uns zu erkennen, wer Gewinner des gesamten Wettbewerbs ist bzw. um welches Buch es geht.

Vergleiche diese Sätze mit dem **nicht bestimmenden Relativsatz:** Hier stehen Kommas vor und hinter dem Relativsatz.

Beispiele:

That young boy, who came first in the 100 m race, also won the swimming competition.
The book by Jack Jones, which is lying on my table, is the one we are using today.
Maggie, who goes to Grove School, is the new table tennis champion.

▶ Wir wissen in diesen Fällen schon, welcher Junge, welches Buch oder welches Mädchen gemeint ist. Die Information im Relativsatz ist zusätzlich.

1 Read the following sentences and put in any missing commas.
If there are no commas missing, put a tick.

EXAMPLE

The guy who sold us the house is quite a nice man. → tick ✔

1. The CD I have just listened to is by Metallica.
2. The Beatles who were a famous pop group split up in the early seventies.
3. Sherlock Holmes who was a very intelligent man solved many difficult cases.
4. The car which he wanted to sell to us had in fact been stolen the night before.
5. The men who were arrested the day before yesterday are responsible for three attacks on British troops. The other men were not connected with the crime.
6. The gun that was used in the murder was found in a nearby river.
7. The prime suspect who was living in Paris at the time was Trevor Sams.
8. The police officer who was carrying an infrared camera was positioned on the roof, whilst the other one watched the road from a car parked opposite the house.

2.6 *Conditional clauses*

REMEMBER

Achtung: Kein would oder will im *if*-Nebensatz. → If I were you, I would not …

When bedeutet nicht das Gleiche wie if:
When beschreibt eine sichere Abfolge, nicht eine, die von Bedingungen abhängt. Es ist ganz klar, **dass** etwas passiert.
Beispiel:
I'm going into town. When I get there, I will buy some food.

If beschreibt eine Sache, die **eventuell** passieren kann bzw. eine Bedingung („wenn" im Sinne von **„falls"**).
Beispiel:
I don't know if I can manage it timewise, but if I get into town I will buy some food.
→ Ich weiß noch nicht, ob ich Zeit habe. Aber **falls** ich es in die Stadt schaffe, werde ich etwas zu essen einkaufen.

Es gibt drei Grundtypen von Bedingungssätzen:
Typ 1: Der Sprecher **hält die Bedingung für erfüllbar.**
Beispiel:
If you give me the money, I will fetch us some ice-cream.

Typ 2: Der Sprecher **zweifelt an der Erfüllbarkeit der Bedingung.**
Beispiel:
If I had the money, I would buy myself a big house.

Typ 3: Der Sprecher **weiß, dass die Bedingung nicht mehr erfüllt werden kann,** weil es sich auf die Vergangenheit bezieht.
Beispiel:
If I had had the money, I would have bought myself a big house.
→ Hätte ich das Geld gehabt, dann hätte ich mir ein großes Haus gekauft.

Besonderheit: ***Mixed conditional***
Manchmal hat die Bedingung, die in der Vergangenheit nicht erfüllt wurde, Wirkung auf die Gegenwart. Dadurch können in einem Satz Formen von Typ 3 und Typ 2 gleichzeitig vorkommen.
Beispiel:
If I had found my wallet yesterday, I would feel a lot better now. → Wenn ich meine Brieftasche gestern gefunden hätte, würde es mir **jetzt** wesentlich besser gehen.

1 Connect the sentences by using conditionals.
Write an appropriate conditional sentence for each situation.

EXAMPLE

They were not in New York that year. That's why they did not visit the World Trade Center.
If they had been in New York that year, they would have visited the World Trade Center.

1. I think it will rain on Saturday. Then I won't need to water the plants.
2. She didn't know her parents were coming. So she did not prepare anything to eat.
3. They are not interested in the house. So they won't look at it.
4. We didn't know you were in town. That's why we didn't call you.
5. When you were young, you never practised the piano. Now you regret this.
6. Why don't you give me your address? Then I can visit you.

2 Translate the following sentences into English.

1. Wenn er den Zug verpasst hätte, hätte er den Job nicht bekommen.
2. Wenn mein Onkel am Sonntag kommt, wird meine Mutter ihren berühmten Apfelkuchen machen.
3. Ich würde mich freuen, wenn unsere Mannschaft morgen gewinnt.

2.7 *The passive*

REMEMBER

Falls der Verursacher einer Handlung nicht feststeht oder nicht erwähnt werden muss oder darf (was häufig in Zeitungsberichten der Fall ist), ist es im Englischen stilistisch eleganter, das Passiv zu verwenden.
Beispiele:
Someone stole his car last night. → His car was stolen last night.
A bottle was thrown out of the classroom window. I've been told that you threw it.
The prisoners were released yesterday at the border.

Das Passiv wird aus einer Form von be sowie dem *past participle* gebildet.
Beispiele:
They **were taken** to the hospital.
The song **was written** in 1969.
Bei Modalverben wird das Passiv gebildet aus: *modal* + be + *past participle.*

Beispiele:
They **can be** beaten.
We **should be** congratulated on that victory.

Verben mit zwei Objekten – z. B. **give**
Aktivsatz: Mike gave her a nice bunch of flowers.
Im Aktivsatz hat das Verb give zwei Objekte (her und bunch of flowers).
Passivsatz: She was given a nice bunch of flowers.
Wer die Blumen gegeben hat (Mike), wird nicht mehr erwähnt. Im Passivsatz wird das Indirektobjekt aus dem Aktivsatz (her) zum Subjekt (She).
"She was given ...". Das klingt wesentlich besser als: "A nice bunch of flowers was given to her".

Andere Verben mit zwei Objekten:
ask offer pay show teach tell
Beispiele:
She was asked several interesting questions.
He was offered a job as assistant teacher.
He was taught English by a native speaker.

Übersetzung von Passivkonstruktionen
Manche englische Passivkonstruktionen werden im Deutschen aktiv übersetzt, und zwar häufig mit „man".
We should have been told. → Man/Jemand hätte es uns sagen sollen.
She could have been given another chance. → Man hätte ihr noch eine weitere Chance geben können.

1 Transform the following sentences into the passive.
Remember: Use the same tense as in the given sentence.

EXAMPLE

Nobody has ever told me not to download these files.
I've never been told not to download these files.

1. Someone gave him the keys, so he let himself in.
2. They didn't invite him to the party.
3. How much will you pay me for the job?
4. When we arrived at the airport we found that they had cancelled our flight.
5. This is a serious problem. We must do something about it now.

2 **Translate the following sentences into English.**

1. Er wurde gezwungen, das Geld zu übergeben.
2. Sie wurden herumgeführt.
3. Es wurde ihnen gesagt, wo sie schlafen konnten.
4. Sie wird ins Krankenhaus gebracht werden.
5. Wir könnten von meiner Tante unterrichtet werden.

2.8 *Reported speech*

REMEMBER

Achtung: Die Zeitverschiebung ***(backshift)*** ist nötig, wenn der einführende Satz in der Vergangenheit steht (He said ...).
Hier ist eine kurze Liste wichtiger Änderungen:
am → was, will → would, have been → had been, was → had been, taught → had taught, must → had to
Might, should, would, could bleiben, wie sie sind.
here → there, this → that, today → on that day

Wenn du eine **direkte Frage als indirekte Frage** wiedergibst, dann ist die **Satzstellung des wiedergegebenen Fragesatzes wie die eines Aussagesatzes.**

What **do you do?**	→ He wants to know **what I do.**
What time **is it?**	→ He wanted to know what time **it was.** (mit *backshift*)
Do you like her?	→ He wanted to know if **I liked** her.

1 **Put the following sentences into reported speech. Use backshift where necessary.**

EXAMPLE

What does she want?
He wants to know what she wants.

1. Where is the toilet?	Do you know
2. Do you know him?	He wanted to know
3. What's his name?	She couldn't remember
4. Why didn't he come?	We wondered
5. When will the show begin?	He wanted to know
6. I won't come.	She said (that)
7. They don't stand a chance.	He told us that
8. It hasn't rained for ages.	They informed us that

9. I don't want to live here. She complained that ______
10. Who is this child? They had no idea ______

2.9 *Prepositions*

REMEMBER

Präpositionen drücken das Verhältnis zwischen Personen bzw. Dingen aus. Welche Präposition welches Verhältnis in welchem sprachlichen Kontext ausdrückt, muss gelernt werden.

Lerntipp:
Übersetze die folgenden Sätze ins Deutsche. Schreibe dir unbekannte Wendungen auf und lerne sie. Präpositionen sind (nicht nur im Englischen) eine der häufigsten Fehlerquellen.

▶ **at**

I am **good/hopeless at** German.
Is he **at work?**
Let's meet **at the opera house.**
She drove **at 90 miles** per hour.
At the end of the road.
Open your book **at page** nine.
The children are **at play.**
I saw him **at the doctor's.**
He is not **at school** today.
They were waiting **at the bus stop.**
He left school **at the age of 16.**
Water boils **at 100 degrees.**
At the top/bottom of the page.
Remember: The exercise is **on** page nine.
What are you **driving** at? (andeuten)
Now **look at that.** /Take a **look at that.**

▶ **in**

She is **in love.**
In a car (But: **on** a plane/train/ship)
We arrived **in Spain/Madrid.**
(But: We arrived **at** the airport.)
I still believe **in God.**
They **succeeded in** finding her.
You must pay **in cash.**
He's **in prison/in hospital.**
She's always **in a hurry.**
In the news
I **came in** my car.
He **specialised in** second hand cars.
How much is that **in euros?**
He is **interested in** cars.

▶ **on**

I found it **on the Internet.**
He was **on television**/on the radio.
Is he still **on the telephone?**
We went **on a trip**/journey.
On the whole I liked the show.
I'm **on a diet.**
We put him **on the train**/plane/ship.
She was **on the same programme.**
They went **on strike.**
I'm here **on business.**
He did it **on purpose.** (absichtlich)
The house is **on fire.**

He went there **on foot.**
It all **depends on** you.
Try and concentrate **on the text.**
I **insist on** her having a haircut.

He **blamed** the accident **on** me.
Can I **rely on** you?
He **spent** all his money **on** whisky.
You **are on** now. (It's your turn.)

▶ **by**

She took him **by the hand.**
It was **sent by post.**
Contact me **by e-mail**/telephone.
Numbers **have risen by** ten percent.
Did you travel **by car? (No, on foot)**
(But: Actually, I came **in** my car today.)

I found him **by accident.** (per Zufall)
You should learn it **by heart.** (auswendig)
Can I **pay by credit card**/cheque?
He **won by a split second.**
I was **surprised by (at)** that.
He was **impressed by (with)** her.

▶ **for**

What's the **reason for** this?
What can you **use this for?**
Have more **respect for** others.
Did you **pay for** the meal?
She **took the blame for** it.
I am **sorry for** what I did.

What are you **waiting for?**
Would you **care for** a cup of tea?
He was **asking for trouble.**
Did you **pay the bill?**
What did you **do that for?**
Did he **apologise for** what he did?

▶ **of**

That was **nice/stupid of** you.
I am **proud of** us.
I am painfully **aware of** it.
This is **typical of** her.
Are you **sure of (about)** that?
The pool was **full of** water.
(But: They **filled it with** water.)

What do you **think of** that?
Are you **jealous of** me?
He is sick and **tired of** listening to his dad.
They are **scared/afraid of** him.
I will always **think of/about** you.
Can you **make use of** this/him?
I can't **think of** his name.

▶ **from**

He **suffered from** a serious illness.
Keep away from the dog. It bites.

This will **protect you from/against** the rain.
He **came from** Russia.

▶ **about**

They just don't **care about** others.
Did you **think about** it?

We had a **discussion about** it.
(But: We **discussed the whole issue.**)

▶ **to**

We **went to a party.**
What **happened to** the old man?

We **were invited to** a party.
That's terrible. How did it **come to that?**

1 Put in the right preposition.

1. She is brilliant ______ English.
2. The box was full ______ gold.
3. You can't blame Jack ______ it.
4. My aunt suffers ______ cancer.
5. Oil prices have risen ______ 30 per cent.
6. They went there ______ their car.
7. They can't protect you ______ the Mafia.
8. They did it ______ purpose.
9. That's typical ______ their way of life.
10. Sorry. How stupid ______ me.
11. There is a new book out ______ skiing.
12. Show more respect ______ her.
13. Can I send my application ______ e-mail?
14. He was jealous ______ him.
15. They asked her ______ help.
16. I was invited ______ Ella's party.

2 Translate the following sentences into English.

1. Der Grund für dieses Missverständnis ist, dass er kein Englisch kann.
2. Der Roman wurde von William Faulkner geschrieben.
3. Das war nicht sehr klug von dir.
4. Er ist sehr gut in Musik. Alle sind sehr von seinem Spiel beeindruckt.
5. Hat dich das überrascht?
6. Ich glaube, ich sollte eine Diät machen (auf Diät gehen).
7. Sie baten mich um Unterstützung.
8. Sie schickten die Unterlagen (= documents) mit der Post.
9. Glaubst du an Wunder?
10. Ihr könnt stolz auf euch sein.
11. Guck mich nicht an! Ich suche nur meine Schlüssel.
12. Ich bin heute nicht da. Kannst du dich darum kümmern?

2.10 *Phrasal verbs*

REMEMBER *Trouble spots*

Phrasal verbs (zusammengesetzte Verben) sind eine Kombination aus Verb + Präposition oder Adverb. Die Bedeutung eines *phrasal verb* ergibt sich manchmal aus der Bedeutung seiner einzelnen Bestandteile (z. B. listen to someone, look for something), aber sie ist in den meisten Fällen idiomatisch, d.h. sie kann nicht einfach aus der Bedeutung der einzelnen Teile erschlossen werden.

Beispiele:

Look out! That tree is falling over.	→ Pass auf!
Can you look after the kids while I go to the shops?	→ aufpassen auf
Jack looked in yesterday and asked after you.	→ reinschauen
If you don't know a word, look it up in the dictionary.	→ nachschlagen
She looked him over and turned him down.	→ sich jmdn. anschauen
They called it off.	→ absagen
I can't stand it.	→ es nicht aushalten können
He dropped out of school.	→ von der Schule abgehen

Phrasal verbs werden von Muttersprachlern (vor allem in der gesprochenen Sprache) gern verwendet und sollten von dir verstanden werden. Wenn du sie - an der richtigen Stelle - benutzt, machen sie dein Englisch idiomatischer und verbessern damit deine Ausdrucksweise.

1 **Replace the phrasal verb with the appropriate verb or expression from the box.** You may have to put the verb in the right tense.

avoid *separate/divorce* *manage* *see* *succeed*
cancel *reduce speed* *continue* *increase speed*
agree *invent*

EXAMPLE

He dozed off in the lesson.
→ *fell asleep*

1. There was a lot of traffic, so I had to slow down. →
2. OK, I'll go along with that. →
3. Jenny's parents have split up. →
4. The flight has been called off. →
5. It's getting late. Come on, speed up a bit. →
6. I think this story has been made up. →
7. I came across John the other day in the pub. →
8. He went on talking and talking. It was horrible. →
9. You wouldn't believe it, but they pulled it off. →
10. They didn't earn a lot of money, but they got by. →
11. I said I'd go and I can't get out of it now. →

2 Rob's e-mail

Read the following text. Underline the phrasal verbs. Do you understand them? Can you translate them into German?

Hello Everybody,

This is Rob again, straight from Amsterdam. Jack and I are really turned on by this fantastic city. We are staying at a rather run down hotel, with the paint coming off everywhere. It's nice enough really, but they should do it up soon or it might be shut down. And the place is really crammed, so we have to share our room with five Americans. Well, as a budget traveller you can put up with that kind of thing. We did complain though, when it turned out that Jack didn't even have a proper bed. We went to see the manager and knocked the price down from 25 euros to 15 per night.

So our room is really full, but we are getting along fine, except that last night things got a bit out of hand. It was our next door neighbours. They were having a lot of drinks and one of them passed out on the stairs. Fortunately he didn't throw up but it was quite an off-putting sight.

Anyway, when we asked the guys to cut down the noise (at three in the morning) they told us to push off. They also set off the fire alarm, because they all went on smoking, although they had been told off by the staff at least twice.

It turned out that they were football supporters from Germany. The next day Germany was up against Holland and lost three nil. Serves them right!

Our German friends felt a bit down when they came back to the hotel, so we tried to cheer them up. Actually, it worked out OK and in the end we got along quite well with them. However, when they wanted to carry on drinking, we left for a rock concert in the city centre which turned out to be a terrific event.

Cheers from A'dam

Rob

PS: At the concert there was a guy trying to rip off some tourists by selling them overpriced tickets - for a concert that was free in the first place! It was fun to see the police running after him, but they couldn't catch up. He was really fast, so he just got away with it.

2.11 *Spelling*

REMEMBER **Pluralbildung/Steigerung/Formen des Verbs**

Ein Wort endet mit einem Konsonanten +y: → ies/ier, iest/ied

Beispiele:

story → stories baby → babies lucky → luckiest scary → scarier, scariest

carry → carries → carried hurry → hurries → hurried

Konsonantenverdoppelung gibt es vor -ed und -ing, wenn die Betonung auf der letzten Silbe liegt.

Beispiele:

begin → beginning prefer → preferred regret → regretting

stop → stopped occur → occurring hit → hitting

1 **Write down the correct version of the verb. Tick the gap if the spelling is OK.**

1. He preferred ______ to walk me home after the party.
2. When I watched them they were winning ______.
3. I studyed ______ Spanish.
4. She worryed ______ about her daughter.
5. He wore a hand-knitted ______ pullover.
6. "Stop spliting ______ hairs", she said.

2.12 *A mixed bag of trouble spots*

GOOD TO KNOW **Typische Fehler**

Hier findest du eine Sammlung häufig vorkommender Fehler.

Slips of the pen **(Verwechslungen/Verschreiber)**

It wasn't ~~there~~ fault. → their

~~Its~~ wrong. → It's

He is taller ~~then~~ his brother. → than

They are her two ~~sister's~~ → sisters

It's my ~~brothers~~ bike. → brother's

I always ~~loose~~ my keys. → lose

He was ~~choosen~~ by the jury. → chosen

I don't like ~~beeing~~ told what to do. → being

Please be ~~quite~~. → quiet

He ~~cought~~ the criminal. → caught
I've known him all my ~~live~~. → life
The concert was broadcast ~~life~~. → live

Wrong usage **(falscher Gebrauch)**

Make/do something

She forgot to ~~make~~ her homework. → to do homework
They ~~made~~ a good experience. → to have an experience
We are ~~making~~ an interesting project. → to do (work on) a project
Let's ~~make~~ a survey. → do/carry out a survey
She really ~~makes~~ a good job. → to do a job
They ~~make~~ their work very efficiently → do their work
We are ~~making~~ a party on Saturday. → having a party
He is still ~~doing~~ the same mistakes. → to make a mistake
It's difficult to ~~find~~ friends here. → to make friends.
He always ~~does~~ an effort. → to make an effort

1 Translate the following sentences into English.

1. Bitte sag mir deinen Namen.
2. Ich habe es ihm gesagt.
3. Gestern bekam ich einen wundervollen Nachtisch.
4. Ich will Pilot werden.
5. Das war eine schwere Aufgabe.
6. Die Kiste war zu schwer für mich.
7. Ich werde morgen in die Schweiz fahren.
8. Ich will jetzt nicht rausgehen.
9. Ich möchte gern zwei Postkarten.
10. Kannst du uns einen Tee kochen?
11. Das Wasser kocht.
12. Mein Vater kocht gern.
13. Lass mich bitte schlafen.
14. Mein Wochenende war furchtbar. Meine Eltern ließen mich die Garage putzen.
15. Kannst du mich zum See bringen?
16. Wir haben ein Haus am Meer.
17. Er gewann den ersten Preis und bekam eine gute Note in Physik.
18. Er hat einen guten Preis für sein Auto bekommen.
19. Ich interessiere mich für Technik.
20. Seine Technik ist großartig. Er ist wirklich ein brillanter Fußballspieler.
21. Wenn du jetzt nicht gehst, dann gibt es Ärger.

22. Wenn ich nach Hause komme, trinke ich immer einen selbstgemachten (= home-made) Milkshake.
23. Ich konnte die Hausaufgaben nicht machen.
24. Stockport ist bei Manchester.
25. Was ist deine Meinung? Was denkst du?
26. Das sind großartige Neuigkeiten.
27. Der Chef ist heute krank. Herr Schmidt, können Sie bitte übernehmen?
28. Wir haben heute ganz viele Laster überholt.
29. Seid ihr fertig (= mit euren Aufgaben)?
30. Seid ihr fertig (= bereit, etwas zu tun)?

2 Translate the following sentences and the "false friends".

EXAMPLE

He works in a gymnasium. ≠ dt: Gymnasium = grammar school
Er arbeitet in einem Fitnessstudio / einer Turnhalle.

1. She is just an ordinary woman. ≠ dt. ordinär
2. Who is the chef here? ≠ dt. Chef
3. Are you going to overtake that lorry? ≠ dt. übernehmen
4. He was such a brave boy. ≠ dt. brav
5. She blamed herself. ≠ dt. sich blamieren
6. Come on now, be sensible. ≠ dt. sensibel
7. I overheard their conversation. ≠ dt. überhören
8. Can I get a receipt for the medicine? ≠ dt. ärztliches Rezept, Kochrezept
9. She was very sympathetic when I told her about my problem. ≠ dt. sympathisch

REMEMBER *So/such (a)* (so/so ein)

Auch bei *so/such (a)* treten häufig Fehler auf:

He is ~~so~~ a silly boy. → He is such a silly boy.
Crisps contain ingredients ~~so~~ as salt and vinegar. → ... such as salt ...
We have ~~such a wonderful weather.~~ → ... such wonderful weather

such (a) (so ein/solch ein)

- steht mit einem Nomen → I have never read **such a book** before.
- oder einem Adjektiv + Nomen → She is **such a strong girl.**

so

- steht mit einem Adjektiv oder Adverb → You are **so** beautiful. → She ran **so** fast.

3 Translate the following sentences into English.

1. Sie ist ein so süßes kleines Mädchen.
2. Wir hatten so ein schreckliches Wetter.
3. Hast du jemals ein so hohes Gebäude gesehen?
4. Wie kann man nur so vergesslich sein?
5. Solche Leute mag ich nicht.

REMEMBER *Meaning/opinion* (Meinung, Bedeutung)

To mean: meinen, beabsichtigen
Meinen: What do you mean? → Was willst du sagen?
Bedeuten: This means that we can't go. → Das heißt/bedeutet, dass ...
Beabsichtigen: I didn't mean to hurt you. → Ich wollte dir nicht weh tun.

Achtung: Meaning bedeutet nicht das Gleiche wie das deutsche „Meinung". Dafür musst du opinion verwenden.
Meaning: Bedeutung oder Wichtigkeit
Beispiele:
The meaning of this word is ...
We talked about the meaning of life.
Having a baby gave a new meaning to her life.

4 Translate the following sentences into German.

1. Robbing a bank could mean years of imprisonment if you get caught.
2. I didn't mean to be impolite.
3. Sorry, but I didn't get your meaning.
4. He didn't mean to come home so late.
5. Well, what's the meaning of all this?
6. Does this mean that you can't come?
7. Winning the cup final gave her handball career a new meaning.
8. What do you mean by that?
9. This means that we won't be going to the match.

REMEMBER *Articles* (Artikel)

Folgende Übersicht zeigt, wann der bestimmte Artikel verwendet wird und wann nicht.

Artikel:	kein Artikel:
→ **etwas Bestimmtes**	→ **etwas Allgemeines**
z. B. ein Gebäude (the school)	z. B. Schule als Institution
I like **the school** (building).	I like **school** (in general).
The life of children in the 19th century ...	**Life** in the 19th century was hard.

Mit oder ohne Artikel: Bedeutungsunterschiede

I have to go to the hospital.	I have to go to hospital.
→ Ich arbeite dort, oder besuche jemanden.	→ Ich bin krank.
She is going to the school.	He goes to school.
→ geht dort hin, z. B. als Mutter	→ Er ist Schüler.
I am going to the church.	I go to church on Sundays.
→ geht zu dem Gebäude, z. B. Besichtigung	→ Gottesdienst/ist ein Gläubiger
I am in the office today.	He is in office.
→ Ich bin im Büro.	→ Er ist im Amt (z. B. als Minister).
He goes to the prison every Sunday.	He is going to prison.
→Er besucht jemanden oder arbeitet dort.	→ Er ist ein Straftäter.
We don't have the space for it.	They were lost in space.
→ Raum im Sinne von „Platz"	→ (Welt)raum
They walked over to the bed.	They went to bed.
→ zum Bett hin	→ zu Bett (schlafen) gehen

5 **Put in *the* where necessary.**

A mother talking to her children early in the morning:
Come on you two. Get ready. You should be off to ______ school by 8.30. By the way, how was ______ school yesterday? Did you get much homework? Anyway, I'm going to see Mr Jenkins about your grades. So I'll be at ______ school at about 10.30.

A father later in the evening:
Oh yes, ______ life is certainly hard at times. At least ______ life of your Dad is. I really had a terrible day at ______ work. I spent the whole day in ______ office. I had to do so much work – I couldn't even go to ______ toilet. I'm really tired, so I'm going to ______ bed right now.

A student at school:
Would you believe it, we were in that fantastic town and what did my parents do? They went into ______ church to have a look at the windows. Anyway, when they got

to the place there was a service, and the people who go to ____ church regularly don't like strangers looking at ____ church while there is a service going on. So my mum and dad picked me up at ____ hotel and we went to a museum about ____ life during the French Revolution, especially about ____ life of young people at that time.

6 **Put in *a, the* or no article.**

1. My father had always wanted to become ____ teacher, but now he has started work as ____ electrician with ____ British Telecom.
2. Sandy will not be home for ____ dinner today because she is meeting up with some friends of hers after ____ school and they are all going to ____ cinema.
3. Well, ____ life is difficult for me. But look at ____ life of the big stars. They have such ____ good time.
4. In London I went to ____ really interesting workshop. The teacher was ____ Scotsman. ____ time went by so quickly. I will always remember ____ great time I had when I was there.
5. ____ June is my favourite month. However, ____ June of 2002 was terribly wet. I always got wet on my way to ____ school. We went to ____ Switzerland and ____ Netherlands in ____ summer holidays. That was great. Especially when we stayed at ____ Lake Geneva.

REMEMBER *Comparisons* (Steigerungen)

Mehrsilbige Adjektive werden mit more und most gesteigert, außer diejenigen, die auf -y enden.

7 **Translate the following sentences into English.**

1. Sie ist die berühmteste Frau der Welt. Viele sagen aber, dass sie auch die schwierigste (= difficult oder complicated) sein kann.
2. Tim ist nicht so schnell wie Ann, aber in Basketball ist er besser als sie.
3. Dieses Jahr ist das schlimmste von allen. Alles ist teurer geworden.
4. Wir sind glücklicher als Jack, aber nicht so glücklich wie meine Großmutter.
5. Er ist einer der berühmtesten Schauspieler der Welt, aber nicht so beliebt wie sein Bruder.
6. Mathe wird immer schwieriger.
7. Obwohl er der jüngste Spieler war, schoss er die meisten Tore.
8. Er ist reicher als Bill Gates.
9. Sie bekommen mehr Geld, aber nicht genug, um sich ein noch größeres Haus zu kaufen.

Test

1 Name the right tense.

Which tense ...

1. is used when you want to describe something that is happening while you are speaking? ______
2. describes a completed event in the past? ______
3. deals with events that started or occurred in the past but are still relevant as you speak? ______
4. is used when you want to talk about an action that took place before another one in the past? ______
5. is used when talking about your intentions for the future? ______
6. describes an event which started in the past and is interrupted by another event? ______

You get 1 point for each correct answer. **Your points:** ____ /6

2 Now match the following sentences with the tenses above.

EXAMPLE

They were walking back home when suddenly a terrible storm broke out. → *6*

1. She has always wanted to be a good piano player. → ______
2. When I was young my mother made me wear pink shirts. → ______
3. This week I'm definitely going to have a haircut. → ______
4. They were drinking heavily, thinking of their friend who had died the night before. → ______
5. Can you see it? Over there. The lion is stalking a zebra. → ______

You get 1 point for each correct answer. **Your points:** ____ /5

3 Put in a suitable preposition.

1. He went to England ______ the age of seven, but he'll be back ______ the end of next year.
2. We don't have any time ______ the week. So we'll have to decorate our house ______ the weekend.
3. Bill looked ______ the girl.
4. We can't go to the shops ______ the day, so we'll have to go this evening.
5. The Wilsons will start renovating their house ______ the beginning of May.

6. If you are interested ______ the job, please tell me ______ the end of next week so that I can make the necessary arrangements.
7. He lives ______ a wonderful flat ______ the 18th floor.
8. When she arrived ______ the school she went ______ the head teacher to complain ______ her son's unfair grades. Then she went ______ the classroom and took her child out ______ the lesson.

You get 1 point for each correct answer. **Your points:** ____ /16

4 Put the verb in the right tense.

1. Look at that cyclist over there. He is going far too fast. We ______ (crash) any minute.
2. "Oh dear this box is really heavy." – "Don't worry, I ______ (give) you a hand with it."
3. "Should we go and see this new film?" – "Why not? It ______ (be) on at 8 p.m. at the Odeon."
4. What ______ (you/do) tonight? ______ (you/join) us for a meal?
5. She ______ (live) in California when she was young.
6. How long ______ (you/work) on this machine? It's supposed to be ready by this evening.
7. Where do I live? Well, I ______ (stay) at my uncle's for the time being.
8. Sorry, but you can't have my keys right now. I ______ (need) them.
9. I ______ (do) my homework when suddenly the light ______ (go) out and it ______ (be) dark.
10. He knew he was in trouble. He ______ (see) the man before and he ______ (know) that there ______ (be) no escape.

You get 1 point for each correct answer. **Your points:** ____ /15

5 Translate the following sentences into English. Use participles or gerunds.

1. Ich hasse es, zu spät zu kommen.
2. Ich fand ihn, als er gerade Gitarre übte.
3. Verwirrt wegen der vielen Leute, wollte er gestern nicht vorspielen. (= perform)
4. Da er aus Deutschland kam, war er an kalte Winter gewöhnt.
5. Als er sich den Himmel ansah, wurde ihm klar, dass es bald regnen würde.

You get 2 points for each correct answer. **Your points:** ____ /10

6 Gerund or infinitive? Put in the right form of the verb.

1. Did you manage ______ (get) the money back?
2. I hate ______ (write) a text like this one.
3. Are you interested in ______ (join) a new football team?
4. Did he really stop ______ (smoke) on the motorway?
5. Perhaps it might be a good idea if you stopped ______ (smoke).

You get 1 point for each correct answer. **Your points:** ___ /5

7 Mixed bag: Translate the following sentences into English.

1. Wenn du es jetzt nicht tust, werden wir wirklich Schwierigkeiten bekommen.
2. Ihnen wurde ein Zertifikat überreicht.
3. Ich konnte mich nicht daran erinnern, wann er genau verhaftet wurde.
4. Das ist typisch für diese Art Kunst.
5. Hast du sie gestern im Radio gehört?
6. Was ist der Grund dafür?
7. Sie sind geschnappt worden und müssen ins Gefängnis.
8. Ich habe es euch gesagt.
9. Du bist manchmal so ein Egoist.
10. Das Leben ist manchmal hart, vor allem das Leben junger Menschen.

You get 2 points for each correct answer. **Your points:** ___ /20

8 Replace the underlined words to make the sentence sound more polite.

1. <u>You must not</u> smoke in our kitchen.
2. My mum <u>says that we must</u> go and see Mr Pearson right now.
3. <u>You must</u> spend more time on your homework.
4. My dad <u>says that we must</u> be home by ten o'clock.
5. <u>Must you</u> always take my CDs?

You get 1 point for each correct answer. **Your points:** ___ /5

9 Adjective or adverb? Underline the right word.

1. This tastes really good/well.
2. He is working hard/hardly.
3. Please stop. You are running too fast/fastly for me.
4. She speaks perfect/perfectly German.
5. She speaks German perfect/perfectly.

You get 1 point for each correct answer. **Your points:** ___ /5

10 Position of adverbials. Put the following sentences into English.

1. Sie gingen schnell in die Bank.
2. Gehst du jeden Tag schwimmen?
3. Möchtest du heute Abend Tischtennis spielen?
4. Er hat vor drei Jahren einen Unfall gehabt.
5. Wir werden nächstes Jahr in London ein Haus kaufen.

You get 2 points for each correct answer. **Your points:** ___ /10

11 Defining and non-defining relative clauses. Put in commas where necessary.

1. They bought the car which Ray had recommended to them.
2. John who had just finished high school got the job.
3. Nobody expected the girl who had just finished high school to get the job. She had no practical experience whatsoever.
4. The man who lives next door to us was arrested yesterday.
5. Metallica who were very successful in the 1990s are going on tour once more.

You get 1 point for each correct answer. **Your points:** ___ /5

12 Conditional clauses. Translate the following sentences into English.

1. Wenn er morgen nicht kommt, werde ich mit seinem Bruder sprechen.
2. Wenn es nicht geschneit hätte, wären wir pünktlich gewesen.
3. Ich würde mich freuen, wenn ich etwas mehr Zeit für meine Hobbys hätte.
4. Es wäre nicht so schlimm gewesen, wenn er etwas netter zu uns gewesen wäre.
5. Sie wird es ihm erzählen, wenn sie ihn morgen trifft.

You get 2 points for each correct answer. **Your points:** ___ /10

13 Put the following sentences into reported speech.

1. I don't know him. → He said that ...
2. Can you do me a favour? → She wanted to know ...
3. Will you come to the party tomorrow evening? → He asked ...
4. She could have known about it. → They said ...
5. Have you ever seen such a big fish? → He asked ...

You get 1 point for each correct answer. **Your points:** ___ /5

Your total points out of 117 points: ___

- ▶ More than 99? Very good.
- ▶ More than 87? Good.
- ▶ Less than 58? Have a look at the pages in this chapter again. You CAN do better.

3 Texte verstehen

Das solltest du am Ende der Klasse 9 können:

im Bereich Lesen und verstehen:

- Komplexere Texte (auch Originaltexte) sowohl global (d.h. im Überblick und als Ganzes) als auch im Detail verstehen
- Die folgenden Textsorten kennen und verstehen:
  - diskontinuierliche Texte (z. B. Diagramme, Tabellen, Notizen oder Werbeslogans)
  - längere literarische Texte (z. B. Kurzgeschichten)
  - Sachtexte (z. B. zu landeskundlichen oder wissenschaftlichen Themen)

im Bereich Hören und verstehen:

- Komplexere Hörtexte (auch Originalaufnahmen) sowohl global (d.h. als Ganzes) als auch im Detail verstehen
- Die folgenden Textsorten kennen und verstehen:
  - Interviews, Vorträge (*presentations*), Nachrichtenprogramme (*news programmes*), Hörspiele (*radio plays*)
  - vorgelesene Texte aus den Bereichen Landeskunde und Literatur (z. B. Kurzgeschichten)

GOOD TO KNOW *Working with texts*

Aufgabenformen zum Textverständnis können sein:

- das Anfertigen von strukturierten **Notizen** (*note-making / note-taking*) z. B. in Form eines Diagramms oder einer ***mind map***, entweder für dich oder auch für andere
- **Zusammenfassung (*summary*)**
- **Test zum Ankreuzen (*multiple choice*)**: Hier musst du zwischen richtigen und falschen Aussagen unterscheiden können. Außerdem gibt es in manchen Tests die Kategorie *„not in the text"*.
- **Beantworten spezifischer Fragen (*working with the text*)**
- **Sprachmittlung vom Englischen ins Deutsche oder vom Deutschen ins Englische (*mediation*)**
- **Übersetzung (*translation*)** von einzelnen Aussagen oder dem Gesamttext
- **Bericht (*report*)**
- **Beschreibung (*description*)**
- **Texte in erzählender Form (*creative writing*)**, z. B. Inhalte des Ausgangstextes als Tagebucheintrag *(diary entry)*, Kurzgeschichte *(short story)*, szenische Darstellung *(dialogue, speech)* wiedergeben bzw. bearbeiten, also kreativ umsetzen.

Tipp: Wie du solche Aufgaben **sprachlich** umsetzt, erfährst du in Kapitel 4 („Texte schreiben"). Bevor du also die in diesem Kapitel aufgeführten Aufgaben bearbeitest, solltest du dort nachschauen, damit du das „sprachliche Werkzeug" für die Ausformulierung der Aufgaben hast.

3.1 Lesen und verstehen

GOOD TO KNOW *Reading strategies*

1. *Read for gist* (sich einen Überblick verschaffen)	Lies einen Text erst einmal ganz durch, sodass du einen groben Überblick hast, worum es überhaupt geht und ob du den Text im Großen und Ganzen verstehst. Gibt es Passagen, die du gar nicht verstehst, markiere diese, z. B. am Rand, mit einem Fragezeichen.
2. *Read for detail* (spezifische Informationen herausfinden)	Zunächst musst du die Fragestellung genau verstehen (d.h. diese auch genau lesen), um zu wissen, was gefragt ist. Unterstreiche dazu die entsprechenden Begriffe in den Fragen, damit du die Frage umfassend beantwortest. Beispiel: Describe what advantages India has in its development into a technological society and what problems it has to overcome. Gehe dann den Text durch und markiere (*highlight*) die Textstellen, die zu der Frage passen, z. B. indem du die entsprechenden Schlüsselwörter (*keywords*) unterstreichst bzw. hervorhebst. Tipp: Nimm unterschiedliche Farben für die verschiedenen Fragen. Falls nicht schon vorgegeben, nummeriere die Textzeilen, damit du gegebenenfalls auf einzelne Passagen detailliert hinweisen und so genau am Text arbeiten kannst. (In line 35 the author says that ...)
3. *Intelligent guessing*	Fremdsprachliche Texte enthalten immer Wörter, die man nicht kennt. Du kannst diese natürlich im Wörterbuch nachschlagen. Allerdings solltest du das nur tun, wenn du die Bedeutung des Wortes nicht aus dem Zusammenhang erschließen kannst bzw. das Wort für das Textverständnis absolut notwendig ist. Ansonsten verlierst du viel Zeit. Außerdem macht das Lesen eines Textes wenig Spaß, wenn man ständig ein Wörterbuch in die Hand nehmen muss.

4. *Vocabulary building*	Lies so viel Englisch wie möglich, und zwar das, was dich interessiert. So wirst du deinen Wortschatz automatisch erweitern. (Es bleibt immer etwas hängen, selbst wenn du „nur“ liest.) Du kannst Texte natürlich auch ganz aktiv und bewusst als „Steinbrüche“ für deine eigene Wortschatzentwicklung nutzen, indem du dir Ausdrücke herausschreibst und dir aneignest (z. B. in eigene Texte einbaust). Merke dir Ausdrücke, die du gut verwenden kannst, oder solche, die dir einfach gefallen, weil du sie z. B. witzig findest. (Beispiel: Unfortunately he couldn't make it because he had kicked the bucket. Finde heraus, was das heißt.)

Track 1

Australia's "Stolen Generations": High Time for an Apology

1 First read the text for gist.

You can also listen to the text on the CD.

It took the Australian government decades before the Prime Minister finally issued a formal apology to the so-called Aborigines in February 2008 for what could easily be called one of the most shameful political acts ever carried out in Australian history. What did they have to feel sorry about?
It all started at the end of the 19th century when the Australian government decided to take children out of Aborigine families, if the latter where thought to be incapable of raising their children properly. The children – mainly those of mixed race, but growing up in an Aborigine environment – were then placed either in orphanages (although their parents were not dead) or children's homes, or they were given to white foster parents.
The methods the government institutions used to get hold of the children included cages equipped with spring doors into which young children were lured with trails of sweets, or social workers pretending to give the kids a free ride to church. In other cases, the children were just forcibly removed from their families against the will of their parents. The children were then simply taken away, and many of them never saw their parents again.
The idea behind that was that children were supposed to obtain a better education and grow up in social conditions which would guarantee a better start and enable them to have a career later on. Furthermore, the whole programme was aimed at taking the young Aborigines into "civilisation" by making them familiar with white European values and turning them into "decent, law-abiding Australians". Viewed from a modern perspective,

this can be seen as a rather racist notion, as the white Australian government did not really acknowledge the culture and way of life of the Aborigines. Neither did they respect the rights of Aborigine parents to their children.
Historians estimate that, all in all, at least 100,000 children had been taken away from their families by the time the programme was finally stopped in the late 1960s.
However, it took almost another 30 years, right into the late 1990s, for the whole scale of the programme to be made public. In fact, many Australians knew little about it and had hardly been aware of the turmoil it had created in the Aborigine community. Imagine you were taken away from your family never to see them again, and either put in a home or given to complete strangers. It must have hurt incredibly and it is no wonder that some Aborigine representatives are now calling for more than just a formal apology from the government. They demand financial compensation for the sufferings of the "stolen generations".
So far the government has not responded to such demands.
(Harry Smith, *Sydney News,* 20 February 2008)

2 What is this text about? Write one sentence in answer.
This will be an ultra-short summary – also called an "umbrella sentence" – expressing the essence of the text without any details.

3 Answer the following questions.

1. What does the text say about the white Australians' attitude towards the Aborigines in the late 19th century?
2. What justifications, according to the text, were given by the Australian government for taking Aborigine children away from their families?
3. How did the authorities get hold of the Aborigine children?
4. When did a great number of Australians become aware of the problem?
5. What do some Aborigines want the Australian government to do with regard to the "stolen generations"?
6. Where does the author of the text express his own opinion on the issue?

4 Replace the following words or phrases from the text with other English expressions you know.
Then translate them into German. Learn the new expressions.

EXAMPLE

It took almost another 30 years. → *Almost another 30 years passed/went by.*
Es dauerte noch weitere 30 Jahre.

1. They were supposed to obtain a better education.
2. The programme was made public.
3. They had hardly been aware of it.
4. They are calling for more than just an apology.
5. So far the government has not responded.

5 **Translate the following sentences from the text into German.**

1. It could easily be called one of the most shameful political acts ever carried out in Australian history.
2. The Aborigines were thought to be incapable of raising their children properly.
3. The children were placed either in orphanages or children's homes, or they were given to white foster parents.
4. In other cases, the children were just forcibly removed from their families against the will of their parents.
5. The idea behind that was that children were supposed to get a better education and grow up in social conditions which would guarantee a better start and enable them to have a career later on.
6. Historians estimate that, all in all, at least 100,000 children had been taken away from their families by the time the programme was finally stopped in the late 1960s.

Bush flies. A letter from Australia

Track 2

1 **Read the text.**
You can also listen to the text on the CD.

Good Day Mates (back home and elsewhere),
At least I have got some time left now to drop you a line. Sorry I haven't been in contact for so long, but I was up to my ears not only in work, but, do you believe it, in flies. Little Australian bush flies trying to make their way into your ears, nose and eyes. Honestly, it's driving us nuts, even the Autralians in our group find it most annoying. You wouldn't believe that there could be so many flies in just one place. As I am sitting here out on the veranda with a fashionable flymask covering my face, my jeans and T-shirt are black with the tiny bastards. I mean, they don't bite or do anything really nasty, but they are a real nuisance and make life for everyone quite miserable.

Otherwise, the work on the farm is hard (but not back-breaking) and the people are really friendly and all that. It would be a perfect working holiday if it weren't for those bush flies. You see, I'm quite obsessed with the little crawlies. Actually, we ran into a university professor the other day who told us why it is that Australia has so many flies, most probably a record-breaking level. Here is the story. Hope you find it interesting. (It's definitely more interesting than my work as a farmhand here in the middle of nowhere.)
Now first of all, you might ask yourself where do the little bastards come from. Good question, as it was actually us who brought them to Australia, along with our convicts. Well, we didn't take them to Australia directly, as they were already there, but when the first colonists arrived at the end of the 18th century, they brought a number of cows. Just their luck, for it emerged that the flies felt immensely happy about the cow dung, as it provided an ideal breeding ground for them, making them multiply like wild. Nowadays there are about twenty million cattle in Australia and they each drop about twelve cowpats a day. Can you imagine how much dung that is every day across Australia? Oh, don't think about it. It's massive, and the flies just love it.
So really, at the end of the day, it's due to the cows that Australia has become a fly-infested country (at least in the summer), because before the arrival of the Europeans, the flies had to dwell in kangaroo droppings or what have you. To cut a long story short, there was not so much sh... lying around before we came, so breeding was a great deal harder for the flies.
So what can be done about the nuisance, I hear you ask.
Well, there have been attempts of course to clamp down on the little suckers, but the core of the problem, the presence of some twenty million cows all over the place, still exists, as cattle ranching is an important factor in Australia's economy.
What they did and still keep doing is to breed dung beetles in great numbers. Dung beetles eat dung (logically enough), and if you had enough dung beetles to eat up all the cow dung, or at least a considerable part of it, the bush fly would have fewer opportunities to breed and consequently there would be fewer of them.
That's the theory. But so far, the practice has been more difficult. You just can't produce enough dung beetles to annihilate enough cow dung in order to be a match for the flies. As the Australian dung beetle seems slow at multiplying, they've tried to import beetles from Africa or breed new kinds of dung beetles in laboratories. Interesting job for a biologist, believe me. If anyone really manages a breakthrough in this, the Australians will make him or her a national hero. But so far, the flies are still having a ball all over the place.
And I've had enough of it for the time being, as they are swarming over my hands and laptop while I'm writing this. Time to go back into the house and wait for sunset. Then the flies go to bed and you can enjoy the splendid Australian outback on your own and have a cool beer with your mates.

Love from down under
Peter "The Fly Hater"

2 **You want to write an e-mail about Peter's stay in Australia.**
Make notes and group them in a list.

3 **Write an e-mail to an English speaking friend of yours.**

Tell them about Peter's stay in Australia and what he told you about the bush flies. Write about 170 words. You can start like this:

EXAMPLE

Hi James,
I've just got an interesting e-mail from an old friend of mine, Peter. He writes ....

4 **True, false or not in the text? Correct the wrong sentences.**

1. Australian bush flies are very dangerous to people.
2. Australian bush flies were brought to Australia by the British settlers.
3. Australians have imported dung beetles from Africa.
4. The bush flies could not be killed with modern pesticides.
5. The dung beetle is supposed to eat up the bush flies.
6. Australia has invited biologists from all over the world to help fight the bush flies.
7. At night the flies vanish and people can go out without being pestered by them.
8. Peter wants to travel back to England as soon as possible.

5 **The following rather casual expressions are from Peter's e-mail.**
Put them into more formal English.

EXAMPLE

... to drop you a line
send you a message/letter, write to you

1. I was up to my ears in work.
2. It's driving us nuts.
3. ... multiply like wild.
4. The flies are having a ball.
5. ... from down under.

6 **Replace the following words or phrases from the text with other English expressions you know.**
Then translate them into German. Learn the new expressions.

EXAMPLE

Sorry I haven't been in contact for so long.
Sorry, I haven't written to you (for such a long time.)
Entschuldige, dass ich mich nicht gemeldet habe.

1. They find it most annoying.
2. They are a real nuisance.
3. They make my life miserable.
4. The farm is in the middle of nowhere.
5. It emerged that the flies felt immensely happy about the cow dung.

Track 3

A personal report. Two American high school girls in India

Caroline and her friend Susan, both American, have just moved to New Delhi for an exchange. Here is a report they sent back to their school.

1 Read the text.
You can also listen to the text on the CD.

Hi Everybody,
We've more or less settled into our life in Delhi, so we thought we'd send you another update. If you can't remember (and we have a hard enough time remembering ourselves where we are and what we're doing), we are at Nehru International School. In any case, Nehru is not just the school, but the actual building in which we live and study. There are about ten little apartments for international students, one of which Susan and I inhabit.
The kitchen isn't bad, although we had to add some cooking implements. There's a kettle (i.e. a pot with integrated heating element) to heat water quickly. Unlike English kettles, however, it does not switch off on its own when the water is boiling, so there's an unofficial competition in the building about who can destroy the most kettles by forgetting that they're on (and burning them). Gail from Australia is currently in the lead at two, Christine from the UK in second place with one, while Dowd

from Baltimore threw in the towel and bought a good one after he had burnt one out. We're in pathetic last place with none burned yet, but it's only a matter of time ...

After a strenuous commute of about 30 seconds we make it to the classroom where there are two computers with Internet access. (We actually also have Internet access from our room, but Susan usually uses that.) However, the power goes out about once a day for an hour, so you have to be careful not to lose work. (Side note: Is it just us, or do we always hear in the U.S. how India is some kind of Mecca of technology? Yet here we are at one of India's top schools, and even the teachers have a hard time getting on the Internet regularly.) Nehru International also supplies some daily newspapers and weekly magazines, so at least there's something to read when the power goes out.

Not that we're complaining - when we're homesick, we can go to Pizza Hut. McDonald's, though, doesn't sell 'real' burgers (no beef pretty much anywhere in India), but things like the McAloo Tikki (potato pancake in a bun) and the McMaharaja (some kind of veggie burger).

Honestly, we've only just figured out most things on campus, so we're still exploring things off campus. (That means we're still a bit lonely and dying for news from back home.) One of the fun things, though, is just getting off campus. Our preferred mode of transportation is the scooter rickshaw (called a 'tuktuk'), a little yellow and green vehicle that has the motor of a scooter (I think) but a covered seat in the back that can seat two to three people (if they're good friends). These rickshaws drive around campus randomly (or wait systematically at the campus entrance, but that's a 25-minute walk) and usually stop and ask if you want to go anywhere.

Then, the negotiation starts. Before you even start, you have to make sure they know where you want to go. First, because the drivers don't all speak English and second, because Indian facial expressions and gestures are so different that a confirmation is not always recognizable to us. Then, they give you a price, which is usually about 50-100% too high. (This isn't just our impression - people with lots more experience in India have confirmed this. For one thing, they're obviously starting the negotiation high; for another, we're paying what's known as the 'white tax.') In response, you can laugh and walk away, offer a lower price, or just gawk in amazement. It's a back and forth that's sometimes fun and sometimes just plain annoying when they're clearly trying to rip you off. If you've gone to the market for 20–30 rupees three times and suddenly someone asks for 50 rupees, you know they're messing with you. But we're taking it as a challenge to develop negotiation strategies that end with a fair price!

Anyway, we have to finish our report just now as we are going to meet up with some interesting guys from Germany. We'll tell you more about what we've been discovering here in India next time. We hope you're doing well, and we'd love to hear from you!

CU guys,
Caroline and Susan

2 **Find headings for each paragraph of the text.**

1. paragraph:
2. paragraph:
3. paragraph:
4. paragraph:
5. paragraph:
6. paragraph:
7. paragraph:

3 **Express in your own words what Caroline and Susan say about …**

1. their accommodation.
2. computers and the Internet.
3. McDonald's.
4. travelling around Delhi.
5. negotiating prices.

4 **Mediation**

Summarize Susan and Caroline's report in German. Write 5-6 sentences. Make sure to answer the questions in the box below. Tip: When you mediate you do not translate directly (see also chapter 4.8 of this book).

GOOD TO KNOW | Ein Tipp zur Sprachmittlung *(mediation)*

Achte darauf, dass du folgende Punkte erwähnst, also die typischen W-Fragen beantwortest (Wer? Wann? Wo? Warum? Wie?).

Beispiele:

Wie lange sind Caroline und Susan schon in New Delhi?
Wo/Wie leben sie?
Welche Probleme gibt es?
Wie bewegen sie sich in der Stadt?
Wie kommen sie mit der Situation zurecht, z.B. beim Einkaufen?
Wie geht es ihnen insgesamt?

5 **What do Caroline and Susan mean when they write:**

1. After a strenuous commute of about 30 seconds we make it to the classroom … (l. 21)?
2. … Dowd from Baltimore threw in the towel … (l. 19)?
3. … Indian facial expressions and gestures are so different that a confirmation is not always recognizable to us. (l. 43 - 44)?
4. … people with lots more experience in India have confirmed this … (l. 45 - 46)?

Children stressed out by ads

Track 4

1 Read the text.
You can also listen to the text on the CD.

Researchers have established that children have become direct targets for marketing strategies. On average they might watch as many as 40,000 commercials a year on TV, let alone adverts on the Net or in papers. This way, they are under constant pressure to keep up with images of what they should look like, what clothes they should wear or what else they should have. This, Professor Mankel from Gothenburg University suggests in a widely read essay in “Children Today”, results in many children suffering from stress symptoms you would normally find in adults. Young girls are probably worst hit by the onslaught of advertising campaigns, and more and more often they suffer from depression and lack of self-esteem because they can’t meet the beauty ideals set out by the cosmetic and fashion industries, sometimes with disastrous consequences for their health.

2 **Answer the following questions.**

1. How are children influenced with regard to their beauty ideals?
2. What are the consequences, and why is it that girls are more affected than boys?

3 **True, false or not in the text? Correct the false sentences.**

1. Children have taken an active role in advertising.
2. Children are getting more and more involved in advertising.
3. Their peer group puts a lot of pressure on them about what to wear.
4. Professor Mankel says that teenagers are a lot more under stress than adults.
5. Young girls are often depressed because they don’t look like the people in the ads.

4 **Replace the following expression from the text with a similar one.**

1. a widely read essay
2. lack of self-esteem
3. with disastrous consequences

5 **Mediation: Summarize the text in German.**

Test

An e-mail from New Delhi

Track 5

1 Read the following e-mail from the exchange students in New Delhi, India.
You can also listen to the text on the CD.

Sorry it's been so long since we last wrote. Now things have changed dramatically. It's over 40 degrees Celsius/100 Fahrenheit every day, we've actually had to present some academic work, we were given a kettle that turns itself off when the water boils, and we've developed an exhausting social life. Good times!
So last time we left you hanging as we were about to depart from Nehru campus on an auto rickshaw. There are three main reasons for daring that: shopping, sightseeing, and socializing.
Shopping is probably our least favorite of the three, but obviously cannot be avoided. We talked last time about the places we buy food – but occasionally we have to (or want to) purchase other things as well. In that case, the problem is figuring out where to go. Of course, we could go to one of the many new western-style malls, where we could buy western-style articles at western-style prices. But where's the challenge in that (and who can afford that in the long run)?
The alternative is where things get difficult. India (or at least Delhi) has not (yet) embraced the concept of the supermarket. No Wal-Mart here! Instead, there are separate markets for different categories of products – the electronics market, the furniture market, the clothes market, etc.
Unfortunately, the markets are not named according to their products, but according to their location, so finding each one involves a round of frantically looking through travel guides (not very helpful for that kind of thing), e-mailing acquaintances (who in spite of being people from Delhi, also known as Dilliwallahs, frequently don't have a clue either), and calling friends (which is mostly successful).
For instance, it turned out that the pictures from my new camera took up so much space on my computer that I decided to acquire an external hard drive. So where to go? After the previously described three-step dance, we figured out we needed to go to the computer market at Nehru Place. Things weren't that much easier there: there are about 200 computer stores that appear to have exactly the same stock, each with a 1-2-meter storefront, but no price tags on anything. In front of each store, eight people congregate, shouting at the top of their lungs to get the shopkeeper's attention. Not being able to speak Hindi doesn't help; many Indians at these places don't speak any English at all. And God forbid you want to know something more complicated, like whether the hard drive will work with Caroline's PC as well as with Susan's Mac! By a not very scientific method of elimination (no crowds of more than ten people; no shops that can't tell us prices; no salesperson who has to call somewhere else to find out prices – but sticking with the guy

who actually pays attention to us for more than ten seconds), we finally ended up with a decently priced external hard drive – and had to go home to relax and recover. That was maybe four weeks ago. So far the drive has worked fine!
Then there was the time where our taxi driver couldn't find the furniture market for a bedside lamp for Susan (which we finally had to have assembled out of two other lamps and only realized at home it was lacking an on and off switch), the clothes market where we were able to buy a salwar kameez for Susan (but had to get her belt on the street and take the whole caboodle to a tailor on the parking lot to get the sleeves attached), and other similar experiences. I guess Dilliwallahs just allocate more time for shopping – we get exhausted after each expedition.
Anyway, that's how we're spending some of our time in Delhi. We've also been traveling a little, but we'll tell you about that next time, hopefully in the not too distant future. Let us know how things are going in the rest of the world!

Yours
Susan and Caroline

2 True or false? Tick the correct answers.

1. Caroline and Susan are tired because ...
   - ☐ it is so hot.
   - ☐ they have to work so hard.
   - ☐ they go out so much.
   - ☐ they have just been sightseeing.

2. To Susan and Caroline going shopping is ...
   - ☐ something they are very keen on.
   - ☐ something they really hate.
   - ☐ something that needs to be done.
   - ☐ something they do not find very hard to do.

3. In New Delhi there are ...
   - ☐ many western-style shops.
   - ☐ no western-style shops at all.
   - ☐ only Indian-style supermarkets.
   - ☐ no American fast-food restaurants.

4. Foreigners might have problems finding certain markets in New Delhi because ...
   - ☐ they have no names and they are located in very dangerous areas.
   - ☐ they have names which show what kind of products they sell.
   - ☐ they are not registered in most travel guides.
   - ☐ they are only used by people from Delhi.

5. At Nehru Place there are some 200 computer stores ...
   - ☐ with such a wide range of products that you could hardly decide what to buy.
   - ☐ all having the same prices.
   - ☐ with no labels on their products.
   - ☐ which are all quite small in size.

6. When trying to buy a hard drive for the computer, Susan and Caroline found ...
   - ☐ the Indian shopkeepers very rude.
   - ☐ it difficult to find a shopkeeper who spoke English.
   - ☐ it interesting to talk to the shopkeepers in Hindi.
   - ☐ it easy to get through the crowd in front of the shop.

7. When they finally bought a computer component, it ...
   - ☐ turned out to be of really bad quality.
   - ☐ did not work properly.
   - ☐ functioned all right.
   - ☐ cost a great deal more than anywhere else.

8. When they went to buy other things at different markets it turned out that ...
   - ☐ things were extremely cheap.
   - ☐ there was often something missing.
   - ☐ they had to pay a lot more than Indians.
   - ☐ they could never get what they wanted.

9. The text is written in ...
   - ☐ very formal language.
   - ☐ a rather casual language.
   - ☐ quite a sad tone.
   - ☐ a rather serious way.

You get 1 point for each correct answer. **Your points: ____ /9**

3 Answer the following questions.

1. In what ways is shopping for Caroline and Susan in Delhi different from shopping in the USA? (5 items) (5 points)
2. What is the “three-step-dance”? (3 points)
3. Explain in German: What were the problems with Susan’s salwar kameez? (2 points)

Your points: ____ /10

Your total points out of 19 points: ____

- ▶ More than 16? Very good.
- ▶ More than 14? Good.
- ▶ Less than 9? Have a look at the pages in this chapter again. You CAN do better.

3.2 Hören und verstehen

GOOD TO KNOW *Listening tasks: how should I approach them?*

Es ist normal, dass du bei einem Hörtext nicht alles verstehst. So geht es übrigens auch Leuten, die sehr gut Englisch können, ja sogar Muttersprachlern, wenn sie einen Akzent hören, mit dem sie nicht vertraut sind.
Konzentriere dich auf das, was du verstehst. Dann kannst du den Rest, oder doch vieles, erraten bzw. logisch erschließen (*intelligent guessing*).

Vor dem Hören solltest du dir zunächst die Aufgabenstellung genau durchlesen. Oft kannst du, zum Beispiel bei *true or false*- bzw. bei *multiple choice*-Übungen, schon mit gesundem Menschenverstand gewisse Aussagen entweder als falsch oder als eher unwahrscheinlich ausschließen. Du könntest diese Sätze mit einem Fragezeichen markieren. Dann kannst du dich beim Hören der entsprechenden Textpassage auf die verbleibenden Antworten konzentrieren.

Wenn du selbst etwas schreiben musst, mach dir entsprechende Notizen, z. B. in Form eines Diagramms bzw. einer Mindmap.
Und ... *don't panic*: Du hast die Möglichkeit, dich beim zweiten Hören besonders auf die kniffligen Stellen zu konzentrieren.

Achte auch auf den Ton des Gesagten. Ist jemand nervös, genervt, freundlich oder feindselig? Dies könnte dir Hinweise auf das Gesagte geben.
Auch Hintergrundgeräusche könnten Informationen zur Situation liefern.

Tipp: Wenn du Probleme beim Lösen der Höraufgaben in diesem Buch hast, dann gehe folgendermaßen vor:
Hör dir die Texte, bzw. die Passagen, die dir Schwierigkeiten machen, **in deinem eigenen Tempo** an, z. B. Satz für Satz, so oft wie nötig. Damit trainierst du dein Hörverständnis und du wirst sehen, dass es dir insgesamt bald leichter fallen wird. Denk daran: Übung macht den Meister.

Zusatztraining!
Versuche, so viel wie möglich Englisch zu hören, am besten Dinge, die dich interessieren. Hier einige Vorschläge:

- Hör bzw. schau dir **englischsprachige Radio- und Fernsehprogramme** an, die auch in Deutschland zu empfangen sind. Die Möglichkeiten im **Internet** sind nahezu unbegrenzt, so bietet z. B. die BBC umfangreiche Hörprogramme an, auch für Jugendliche.

- *Audiobooks* (Hörbücher) sind ebenfalls sehr gut geeignet, dein Hörverständnis zu schulen.
- Eine andere Möglichkeit, viel Englisch zu hören, ist die **DVD.** Schau deine Lieblingsfilme auf Englisch - eventuell mit englischen Untertiteln - an.
- *Last but not least:* **Popsongs.** Hör die Songs zunächst an, die Texte findest du sicher im Internet.

Track 6

Peer group pressure – an interview with Kenneth Parker

1 Listen to the interview with Professor Parker about peer group pressure.

Words you might not know yet:
values = Werte

2 Multiple choice
Tick the correct sentences. There may be more than one correct answer.

1. A peer group is people ...
   - [ ] of the same age as the interviewer.
   - [ ] of the same age.
   - [ ] from a similar social class.
   - [ ] you spend your free time with.
2. The interviewer says that many people worry about teenagers ...
   - [ ] having a problem with alcohol.
   - [ ] staying out late.
   - [ ] behaving in a very aggressive way.
   - [ ] stealing things from shops.
3. According to Professor Parker, peer group pressure is a result of young people ...
   - [ ] suffering from stress at school.
   - [ ] having problems with their families.
   - [ ] wanting to stay with the group.
   - [ ] wanting to be different.
4. Professor Parker says that it is quite normal for teenagers to ...
   - [ ] experiment with new hairstyles.
   - [ ] get involved in criminal activities for a while.
   - [ ] train hard to become a pop star.
   - [ ] develop their own way of life.

5. According to Professor Parker teenage peer groups can ...
   - protect you against criminal youths.
   - help you get over periods of uncertainty about yourself.
   - give you some good ideas about morals and values.
   - help you with problems in your family.

6. Professor Parker suggests that parents should support their teenage children by ...
   - keeping up strict rules of behaviour.
   - keeping in contact with their teachers.
   - keeping them inside the family home.
   - keeping in close contact with them.

7. All in all Professor Parker way of speaking shows that he deals with the topic ...
   - in a very subjective, biased way.
   - in a rather balanced, objective way.

3 Questions on the text

Listen to the interview twice. Make notes while you are listening. Then answer the following questions in complete English sentences.

EXAMPLE

What is the interview about?

Your notes: *peer group pressure/problems/what can parents do?*

Your answer: *The interview is about/deals with the problems of peer group pressure and how parents can support their children in such a situation.*

1. What is a peer group?
2. What, according to some people, happens when teenagers join a peer group?
3. Why do teenagers do things in a group they might not have done on their own?
4. Why are parents so irritated about their sons and daughters growing up?
5. Why is the interviewer worried about her daughter?
6. What are the positive aspects of being in a peer group?
7. What can parents do to support their teenage children?

4 What exactly do they say?

Listen to the interview again and finish the following sentences.

1. Today we have with us Professor Kenneth Parker from the University of Sheffield and ...
2. Well, a peer is a person who ...
3. Take for instance ...
4. Sounds quite grim to me. So should parents ...

5. Suddenly the parents discover that their children have grown into teenagers ...
6. Parents should be there ...

5 **Write down a word or a phrase from the interview meaning the same as the following underlined expression.**

EXAMPLE

They come from almost the same social group.
... from a similar social group.

Professor Parker, what precisely is a peer group?

1. Professor Parker, how much of this behaviour can be connected with peer group pressure?
2. I think we could define peer group pressure as the strong wish of a young person to be part of a group of friends.
3. That's a rather complicated question.
4. You know, they don't want to be noticed by everyone, or be different.
5. You see, it is quite normal for a youngster to want to copy their friends.
6. Suddenly the parents find out that their children have grown into teenagers who want to develop their own ideas.

6 **Mediation**

You are talking about peer group pressure in your German lesson. You would like to tell your classmates about the interview. Summarize the main ideas in German so you can answer the following questions.

1. What do parents worry about?
2. What are the advantages and disadvantages of belonging to a peer group?
3. What, according to Professor Parker, should parents do to support their children?

Smoking teens

Track 7

1 **Listen to another part of "Youth Today" where parents can talk to Professor Parker about problems they are having with their children.**
Then answer the following questions.

1. How does Mandy react when Carol asks her to stop smoking?
2. Why should Mandy stop smoking?
3. Which two questions does Carol ask Professor Parker?

2 Multiple Choice

Tick the correct sentences.

1. Professor Parker says that smoking among teens is ...
   - a problem which can be solved easily.
   - is not a big problem anymore.
   - is a fairly complex issue.
   - just a personal problem.
2. The introduction of a smoking ban in public places has ...
   - made smoking very difficult.
   - almost solved the problem.
   - not helped very much.
   - increased the problem.
3. Professor Parker thinks that Mandy might stop smoking if ...
   - nobody in the family ever smoked.
   - Carol stops smoking.
   - Carol really puts her foot down and takes away Mandy's cigarettes.
   - Carol gently explains the dangers of smoking to Mandy.

3 Write down a word or a phrase from the radio talk meaning the same as:

1. ... I'm really under stress.
2. ... when I had a serious talk with her about it.
3. ... she would make the house stink.
4. ... why do young people start (smoking)?
5. I really want her to stop.
6. ... if your child sees that you are trying hard to give up, she might do the same.

4 Write down the expression from the radio talk corresponding to the following German expressions.

1. Hier ist Carol Scott.
2. Neulich (am Abend) ...
3. Nikotin macht extrem abhängig.
4. ... obwohl sie es besser wissen sollte.
5. ... trotz großer Aktionen seitens der Regierung.
6. ... unseren Kindern die Gefahren des Rauchens bewusst zu machen.
7. die Einführung einer Reihe von Einschränkungen
8. öffentlicher Ort
9. eine bewiesene Tatsache
10. eine Anstrengung unternehmen

Staying out late

Track 8

1 **Finish the following sentences. Use the information from the radio talk.**

1. Norman is the father of a ...
2. At school, Trevor ...
3. When asked where he has been Trevor says that ...
4. Norman finds it difficult ...
5. He asks Professor Parker ...
6. Professor Parker says that for young people staying out late is ...
7. With regard to his son, Norman should ...
8. However, Norman has the right to ...

2 **Write down a word or a phrase from the radio talk meaning the same as:**

1. He came home quite late.
2. ... learning what is right and wrong by yourself.
3. You are entitled to know where ...
4. Now if you succeed in finding a fair solution acceptable to both parties ...
5. in case there is an urgent situation, e.g. an accident

3 **Listen again and put the following expressions in the same order as they come up in the text.**

1. doing all right at school
___. no simple solution to this
___. at a reasonable hour
___. reasonable agreement
___. be prepared to
___. staying out late
___. certain amount of freedom
___. find it hard to talk to him
___. no need to worry
___. come home rather late
___. set rules
___. quite honestly

4 **Write down the expressions from the talk corresponding to the following German expressions.**

1. Er macht sich ganz gut in der Schule.
2. Ich fürchte, dazu gibt es keine einfache Lösung.
3. Also sollten Sie bereit sein, ihrem Sohn ein gewisses Maß an Freiheit zu erlauben.
4. ... dann können Sie zu einem fairen Kompromiss kommen.

Friendships

Track 9

1 Listen to the text and answer the following questions.

1. What is Tracy's problem? Write one sentence.
2. What does Professor Parker say about the differences between boys and girls with regard to friendships?
3. To what extent are teenage friendships an important step in people's personal development?
4. What advice does Professor Parker give to Mrs Tremain?

2 Listen to the talk again.
Write down exactly (word for word) what Professor Parker says about the importance of friendships for teenagers.

We all know ...

3 Write down a word or a phrase from the radio talk meaning the same as:

1. She's been together with some really strange people.
2. ... but they are a lot older.
3. ... I'm very worried.
4. As your child becomes an independent adult ...
5. ... with whom they can talk about their ...
6. ... if something is really wrong.
7. ... you must take decisive action.

Teenagers at war (part one)

Track 10

1 Listen to part one of "Teenagers at war". Tick the correct sentences.
There may be more than one correct answer.

1. Betty Schwarz asks if the media have ...
   - ☐ discovered child soldiers as a good topic for selling their products.
   - ☐ invented the topic of child soldiers to sell their products.
   - ☐ introduced the world to a new problem of children at war.
   - ☐ asked children to become soldiers in order to make interesting reports.

2. Robert Chase answers that ...
   - ☐ there are indeed a lot of dramatic reports on child soldiers.
   - ☐ more and more teenagers have started reporting on child soldiers.
   - ☐ the situation of child soldiers in many countries has worsened.
   - ☐ the situation of child soldiers in some African countries has worsened.

3. Robert Chase says that children were used as soldiers ...
   - only in the past 10 years.
   - only in the past 20 years.
   - throughout human history.
   - mainly by the Nazis.

4. According to Robert Chase, child soldiers in general are often ...
   - easy to control.
   - very radical.
   - do as they are told.
   - very efficient.

5. Nowadays most child soldiers are used by ...
   - political leaders.
   - criminals.
   - warlords.
   - desperate governments.

6. Robert Chase says that people nowadays use child soldiers to fight for ...
   - political change.
   - their religious ideals.
   - economic interests.
   - the defence of their country.

7. There are so many child soldiers because certain governments ...
   - need them to fight against criminals.
   - cannot pay adult soldiers.
   - do not care about the situation.
   - are not really in control of their territory.

2 Listening for detail

Finish the following sentences with the original words from the beginning of the interview.

1. This is Betty Schwarz and I'll be talking to Robert Chase from London University ...
2. Is this a new phenomenon or ...
3. Of course there is a ...
4. Yes, you could say that the whole issue ...

3 Write down a word or a phrase from the radio talk meaning the same as the underlined expressions.

1. Yes, you could say that the whole <u>problem</u> has reached a new dimension with more and more teenagers <u>taking part</u> in it.

2. On the other hand, world history if full of examples of children being exploited as soldiers.
3. ... look at the Nazis, who, just before everything broke apart, did not think twice about calling teenagers to arms.
4. But in general, what's the advantage of using children as young as 12 as soldiers?

Teenagers at war (part two) — Track 11

1 Listen to part two of the interview and do the following tasks.
Make notes first, then write complete English sentences.

1. Describe the current problems some African countries are confronted with.
2. Explain the role of local warlords and criminals with regard to the power of central governments in certain African countries.
3. Describe how children are drawn into private armies and why parents find it hard to do anything about it.
4. Explain how leaders manipulate children to remove their fear of fighting.
5. What is being done to stop children becoming child soldiers?

2 Write down the word or phrase from the radio talk meaning the same as the following German sentences.

1. außer Kontrolle geraten
2. Massenarbeitslosigkeit, fehlende Bildung und Hoffnungslosigkeit
3. Recht und Ordnung aufrechterhalten
4. ... die örtlichen Kriegsherren haben die politischen Führer ersetzt
5. ein Vermögen verdienen
6. ... dass es ihnen besser gehen würde als ihren Eltern
7. beschützt durch Zauberkräfte
8. Heime und Waisenhäuser werden gebaut
9. auf der Straße enden
10. definitiv nicht genug, um das Problem zu lösen

3 Listen to the first half of the talk again and underline the expressions which occur in the text.

Youths Today — *child soldiers* — *current political and economic situation* — *out of control*

the core of the whole problem — *They are desperadoes* — *lost its authority*

the fight over resources — *many children get involved*

recognize what they would be drawn into — *would not join such a group*

Test

Deborah Shurer on German-American stereotypes — Track 12

1 Listen to Deborah Shurer and complete the following tasks.

1. Make a list of the stereotypes Americans, according to Deborah, associate with Germany and the other way round.

   Americans on Germany ⟷ Germans on America (10 points)

2. What is "road rage"? (2 points)
3. What is a "gas guzzler"? (1 point)
4. To what extent does Deborah consider these stereotypes to be false? Give two examples for each country.

   Americans on Germany ⟷ Germans on America (4 points)

5. What does Deborah say about SUVs? (2 points)

Your points: ___ /19

2 Listen again and put the following expressions in the same order as they come up in David's talk.

1. typical differences
___. some of the stereotypes
___. sausage and sauerkraut
___. impressed with
2. thought about it
___. will probably know about soccer
___. stuff like that
___. encountered
___. very nice, but superficial
___. they ... won't really mean it
___. in terms of food
___. what you might expect

You get 1 point for each correct answer. Your points: ___ /10

3 **Listen to Deborah's talk again and find the opposites of the following expressions.**

1. similarities between typical Americans and ...
2. a very chaotic country
3. ignorant Americans
4. it's not very seldom/rare.
5. there are only a few people
6. gas prices have decreased

You get 1 point for each correct answer. Your points: ____ /6

4 **Deborah Shurer on German-American stereotypes. Listen and fill in the blanks.**
Write in your exercise book.

Hi, my name is Deborah, I'm from California and I'm going to talk (1) ____ the differences between typical Americans and typical Germans. The problem of course is, (2) ____? I have thought about this a little bit, since (3) ____.

Some of the things the people in the U.S. will say are typical about Germany are (4) ____: beer and sausage and sauerkraut, everybody knows about.

A lot of U.S. Americans think that Germany (5) ____ and are very (6) ____. Or they think it's always very clean and organized and (7) ____, stuff like that. A lot of Americans, if you asked them what they know about – what they think they know about – Germany, it would be things (8) ____. So they are (9) ____ BMWs and Mercedes, and think that you can (10) ____, which isn't (11) ____ anymore, I think.

And then, (12) ____ Americans might know, ... will probably (13) ____.

So there are (14) ____, what I would call stereotypes, that Americans have about Germany.

In the other (15) ____, some of the stereotypes that Germans have about Americans, the one that I have (16) ____ most in my life is that Americans are all very nice, but (17) ____. What do they mean by superficial? To give you an example, they say that Americans will (18) ____ but (19) ____, or say they (20) ____, and then (21) ____ and try to come together they (22) ____.

That's something Germans think about Americans.

I think (23) ______ Germans probably (24) ______ hamburgers, McDonald's and Burger King and (25) ______ and Coke with the U.S., which of course (26) ______ obesity (27), ______ is another stereotype that Germans have of Americans. That they are all (28) ______. And since they are (29) ______ .

And another thing I was thinking about is the (30) ______. You know that Germans think that the U.S. is a very (31) ______, which you can see in things like (32) ______, the power of the NRA , which is the (33) ______, and (34) ______ heard about something called (35) ______, which is when people get so (36) ______ that they just (37) ______ on the highways. Yes, it does happen but it's not very (38) ______.

Anyway, those are some of the stereotypes Americans have about Germans, and that Germans have about Americans. But (39) ______ such stereotypes. Of course there's (40) ______ in Germany who play soccer, but there's also plenty of people who (41) ______. And Germany may be a very organized country, but (42) ______, I can tell you from personal experience.

The other way around ..., yeah there are (43) ______ in the U.S., but there have been school shootings in Germany, too. And (44) ______ in the U.S. because (45) ______ in the last two years or so. And the really big cars, what we call SUVs (Sports Utility Vehicles) aren't being (46) ______ anymore because they are what we call (47) ______, they (48) ______ that you really have to (49) ______, and for a lot of Americans that don't have (50) ______, they can perhaps (51) ______, but they can't (52) ______, because they can't (53) ______.

You get 1 point for each correct answer. **Your points:** ______ /53

Your total points out of 88 points: ______

- More than 74? Very good.
- More than 66? Good.
- Less than 44? Have a look at the pages in this chapter again. You CAN do better.

4 Texte schreiben

Das solltest du am Ende der Klasse 9 können:

- ▷ Briefe zu verschiedenen Anlässen verfassen
- ▷ Statistiken und Umfragen verstehen und beschreiben
- ▷ Bilder und Cartoons beschreiben
- ▷ Personen beschreiben
- ▷ Texte analysieren
- ▷ Stellung zu unterschiedlichen Themen beziehen

GOOD TO KNOW *Writing your own texts* **(Schreibstrategien)**

Im Folgenden wird anhand von verschiedenen Textsorten gezeigt, wie du eigene Texte erstellen kannst. Hauptaugenmerk liegt dabei auf der Versprachlichung: Wie drücke ich etwas auf Englisch aus?

Hinweis: Die meisten hier aufgeführten Formulierungen dürften dir schon bekannt sein beziehungsweise wirst du sie verstehen. Um sie in deine eigenen Texte einzubauen und so deine Schreibkompetenz zu erhöhen, musst du sie dir aneignen,

- ▶ indem du die Übungen in diesem Teil des Buches durchführst,
- ▶ indem du die für dich relevanten Ausdrücke in deinen Vokabelhefter übernimmst und sie lernst,
- ▶ indem du diese Ausdrücke anwendest, z. B. bei der Bearbeitung der Fragen zu den Hör- und Lesetexten in diesem Buch.

Beim Verfassen eines Textes gibt es einen Viererschritt:

1. Das **Sammeln** von Ideen, Argumenten, Fakten, also dein Material, z. B. in Form eines *brain stormings* und/oder von Mindmaps.
2. Das **Ordnen** deiner Materialien, z. B. in Form eines Arbeitsdiagramms (*flow chart*). Dazu gehören auch sprachliche Mittel, z. B. bestimmte Vokabeln oder stilistische Mittel, die den Text gut lesbar machen.
3. Das **Schreiben** des Textes. Je nach Zeit, die dir zur Verfügung steht (Klassenarbeit oder Hausaufgabe?), fertigst du eine erste Textfassung an (*first draft*).
4. Die **Kontrolle und Verbesserung** des Textes (*editing*).
   Hier solltest du Folgendes prüfen:
   - Zeiten: Habe ich sie richtig verwendet?
   - Rechtschreibung: Schwierige Wörter nachschlagen
   - Flüchtigkeitsfehler wie their statt there usw.
   - Wortbedeutungen: Habe ich bestimmte Wörter/Ausdrücke wirklich richtig verwendet (s. *false friends*)?

Wichtig:
- Bilde keine überlangen Sätze.
- Schreibe „einfaches Englisch“, das du beherrschst. Dies gilt für grammatische Strukturen, aber auch für komplexere Ausdrücke.
- If in doubt, leave it out. Ersetze Formulierungen, bei denen du dir unsicher bist.
- Erweitere deine Ausdrucksmöglichkeiten durch das Lernen und Übernehmen von *chunks* (Textbausteinen) aus „guten Texten“ in deine eigenen Texte.

4.1 Briefe verfassen

GOOD TO KNOW *Letters*

Als Textmerkmale hat jeder Brief einen Absender (im Englischen immer ohne den Namen), die Grußformel und eine Schlussformel.
Nach der Grußformel wird (im Gegensatz zum Deutschen) mit einem Großbuchstaben begonnen.
Man unterscheidet zwischen **offiziellen** und **persönlichen** Briefen. Als Sonderform gibt es außerdem den Leserbrief (*letter to the editor*). Sowohl im wirklichen Leben als auch bei Schreibaufgaben in der Schule wird genau darauf geachtet, dass du Briefe **adressatengerecht** formulierst, d. h. „lockerere Formulierungen“ wären in einem offiziellen Brief, z. B. einer Anfrage nach einem Ferienjob, fehl am Platz.

Der persönliche Brief *(personal letter)*
Der persönliche Brief richtet sich an jemanden, den du bereits kennst und zu dem du eine „persönliche“ Beziehung aufgebaut hast, z. B. eine Brieffreundschaft (*pen pal*). Deine Adresse steht rechts oben, allerdings, wie schon erwähnt, ohne Namen. Je nach Bekanntheitsgrad (ihr schreibt euch schon lange) kann die Adresse auch weggelassen werden.
Die Grußformel könnte heißen: Dear John. Dies ist relativ neutral und kann auch verwendet werden, wenn man sich noch nicht so gut kennt oder wenn man an einen älteren Menschen schreibt. Lockere Formulierungen wie Hello John oder Hi John sollten nur verwandt werden, wenn man sich wirklich gut kennt.
Stilistisch kannst du in einem persönlichen Brief/E-Mail umgangssprachliche Formulierungen verwenden, also – wiederum je nachdem, wie gut ihr euch kennt – lockere Formulierungen (My gosh, he was such a bore.), Teilsätze (What a boring week.), Abkürzungen (z. B: CU = See you) oder Symbole (z. B: einen Smiley).

Wichtig: Neben den formalen Merkmalen eines persönlichen Briefs solltest du auch darauf achten, adressatengerecht zu schreiben, also auf den Partner einzugehen. Für Aufgaben in der **Schule** ist es sinnvoll, eine gewisse Neutralität einzuhalten, es also mit Umgangssprache und Abkürzungen nicht zu übertreiben und größtenteils in vollständigen Sätzen zu schreiben.

1 Last year, you stayed with your British pen pal for two weeks. Now it's your turn to invite him or her to stay with you and your family.

Write a personal letter and invite him/her to stay with you for two weeks over the summer holidays.

REMEMBER Der offizielle Brief *(formal letter)*

Der offizielle Brief hat folgende Textmerkmale:
Die **Adresse** (ohne Namen) steht rechts oben.
Dann folgt das Datum (in der Regel rechts), **Name und Adresse des Empfängers** stehen links darunter. Die **Anrede** ist Dear Sir or Madam, wenn man den Namen des Adressaten nicht kennt, z. B. wenn man sich allgemein bei einer Organisation erkundigt. Ansonsten schreibt man Dear Mr/Mrs Kent, wenn man weiß, mit wem man es zu tun hat. (Wenn mann nicht weiß, ob eine Frau verheiratet ist, schreibt man Ms - weil die Anrede Mrs im Englischen ausschließlich für verheiratete Frauen gebraucht wird.) Stilistisch wird von dir erwartet, dass du dich höflich und neutral, also nicht umgangssprachlich, ausdrückst. So solltest du z. B. keine Kontraktionen verwenden (don't), sondern die Worte auseinander schreiben (do not).

2 True or false? Correct the false sentences.

1. In a personal letter you should use formal language only.
2. Start all formal letters with "Dear Sir or Madam".
3. In a formal letter, the address (but not your name) is put in the top right corner.
4. Name and address of the receiver are put below the address of the sender.
5. You can end an informal letter with "CU" or "love".
6. Americans don't mind if you use casual language in an official letter.
7. In an informal letter you should not use contractions such as don't.
8. For school purposes you should not use too many abbreviations or incomplete sentences, even if you are asked to write a personal letter.
9. In a formal letter you always refer to the addressee as Sir or Madam.
10. If you don't know whether a female addressee is married or not, you address her as Ms.

GOOD TO KNOW | **Wendungen für das Verfassen von Briefen**

- **Anfragen *(requests)***
  I would like to know if ...
  I would be interested to know if/when/what ...
  Could you please let me know if/when/what ...
  I would be grateful if you could ...

- **Kritik, Beschwerden (*criticism/complaints*)**
  Remember: Vergiss auch bei berechtigter Kritik nicht die Höflichkeit.
  I want to/feel I must complain about the quality of the food in your hotel.
  Furthermore I would like to point out that there were no towels in the bathroom.
  I am sorry to say that the facilities were not of an adequate standard.
  The shower did not work properly.
  The teacher was often late and seemed rather unprepared.

- **Höflich nein sagen (*saying no in a polite way*)**
  Dein englischer Austauschstudent schreibt, dass er mit euch am Wochenende eine Fahrt zu einer Sehenswürdigkeit machen möchte. Deine Familie und du haben aber weder Lust noch Zeit.
  Anstelle von "No, that's not possible." oder "We can't do that." kannst du folgende Wendungen gebrauchen:
  That's quite a good idea, but I'm afraid we can't go that weekend.
  The problem is that we are all very busy.
  You see, I don't really know how to get there ...
  Yes, we could possibly do that. But I doubt if everyone wants to come along.
  Dein Austauschpartner will ins Konzert/Kino mit dir, aber du hast eigentlich keine Lust:
  I'm not too keen on that kind of music/film.
  Really, it's not my cup of tea.
  It's not really my idea of a night out. I'd rather stay at home.
  You see, I don't particularly like hip hop music/horror movies.
  Well, I'd rather not go out on Friday. I've got so much work to do.
  I'd really much rather go to the shops with you on Saturday.

3 You would like to spend three weeks at a language school in Great Britain over the summer holidays.

Write a formal letter to the school and ask about their programme (e.g. what activities they offer) and their fees, and tell them about your knowledge of English.

4 An unwelcome invitation. Correct the reply given below.

An American friend invites you to meet him at the local rabbit breeders' show ...

Dear friend,

what a nice idea to meet at your local rabbit club exhibition. Thank you for the invitation. But I'm afraid public transport doesn't provide proper services on Saturdays. Anyway, instead of looking at different rabbits – which I'm not too keen on – I'd really much rather meet you in Washington where we could visit the newly opened Sea Life Exhibition and later on watch the movie "Shark V". I hope you'll also find my suggestion interesting. Looking forward to hearing from you. CU Markus

4.2 Statistiken/Umfragen beschreiben

GOOD TO KNOW *Statistics and surveys*

Für die Versprachlichung bzw. Beschreibung kannst du folgende Formulierungen gebrauchen:
The statistics say that for most of the children in London the situation has improved. (Achtung: „Die Statistik" steht im Englischen fast immer im Plural.)
However **from other statistics we can conclude that** the situation has worsened.
This **survey clearly shows/demonstrates** that more and more teenagers have an alcohol problem.

According to a recent survey, only a **minority** of people could think of a life without cars and electricity.

The **majority** of the employees are prepared to fight for better working conditions.
The survey seems to suggest that things have improved.
There is/are not enough data to support this assumption.

These statistics are in the form of a bar chart (Balkendiagramm), the others are presented as a **pie chart** (Tortendiagramm).

From 1995-2008 there seems to be **a sharp increase** in the unemployment rate.
The percentage of people out of work has risen.
If you compare the figures with those for 1987 you can see that there has been **a moderate increase** in the number of people buying their own houses.
There has been **a slight decrease in the** suicide **rate**.
There has been a considerable **decline in the number** of students.

The **number of people** wanting to move to the inner cities **declined steadily** between 1978 and 1988.
However, in the last twenty years the number of people wanting to buy a house in the inner cities **has risen sharply**.

1 Translate the following sentences into English.

1. Diese Statistik sagt, dass es einen starken Anstieg der Kriminalität gibt.
2. Die Zahl der Arbeitslosen hat sich verringert.
3. Aus dieser Statistik können wir schließen, dass das Problem noch nicht gelöst ist.
4. Es gibt nicht genug Daten, die diese Annahme stützen könnten.
5. Die Mehrheit der Menschen kann nicht ohne ihr Auto auskommen.

2 Find the right word.

1. A systematic collection of facts and figures is called ______.
2. When people go round and ask a lot of other people their opinion on a certain topic, they are conducting (doing) a ______.
3. If numbers are going up there is an ______.
4. If numbers are going down there is a ______.
5. More than 50 % of the population is the ______.
6. Less than 50 % of the population is the ______.

4.3 Die allgemeine Bildbeschreibung

GOOD TO KNOW *Describing a picture*

Die Beschreibung eines Bildes kann entweder eine Aufgabe für sich darstellen oder aber auch ein Teil einer Aufgabe sein, z. B. bei der Interpretation eines Zeitungsartikels, zu dem auch ein Bild gehört.

Zur genaueren **Beschreibung eines Bildes** sind folgende Formulierungen hilfreich:
There are several kinds of picture: drawings (Zeichnungen), paintings (Gemälde), photos, illustrations, advertisements, posters.
People who create pictures: artists, draughtsmen (am. Engl.: draftsman (Singular); meist ein industrieller/technischer Zeichner), photographers
Achtung: Drawer heißt Schublade und drawers kann, im altmodischen Sprachgebrauch, sogar die Unterhose bezeichnen. Gemälde werden von painters, artists (Künstler) gemacht.
Photographers **take** pictures (not ~~make~~).

Achtung: der (Zirkus)artist ist ein artiste oder ein acrobat.

This picture shows/depicts a group of ... (zeigt/stellt dar)
In the picture ...
In the foreground there is ...
In the background you can see ...
In the centre of the picture/painting ...
In the top left-hand corner you can see ... (In der oberen linken Bildecke ...)
In the bottom right-hand corner ... (In der unteren rechten Bildecke ...)
At the bottom/base there is ...

Für die **Interpretation eines Bildes** helfen dir die folgenden Formulierungen weiter:
The whole picture shows/describes/depicts the situation of poor people in London.
All in all the photo shows that life for them is very difficult.
The light colours used by the artist make the building look very impressive.
The dark colours have a very frightening effect on the observer.
They symbolise the fact/idea that ...
The horse you can see in the background probably has some symbolic meaning.
It might stand for ... /It might represent ...
The fact that the girls are facing each other could mean that ...
The fact that the boy is looking in the opposite direction could show that he ...
The expression on the old lady's face shows that she is ...
The posture (Körperhaltung)/body language of the man shows that he is ...

1 **Describe the picture below.**
What do you see? Where are the objects?

2 **Translate the following sentences into English.**

1. Dies hat eine beängstigende Wirkung auf den Betrachter.
2. Der Künstler hat diese Farben gewählt, damit das Bild noch eindrucksvoller aussieht.
3. Dieses Symbol könnte für das Vereinigte Königreich stehen.
4. Sein Gesichtsausdruck und seine Körpersprache zeigen, dass er wütend ist.
5. Das alte Schloss in der oberen Bildhälfte stellt vielleicht die Macht des Königs dar.
6. Das Herz wird hier als Symbol der Liebe benutzt.
7. Auf diesem Bild von da Vinci sieht man eine unbekannte Frau.

4.4 Cartoons beschreiben

GOOD TO KNOW *Describing a cartoon*

Cartoons bestehen aus einer humorvoll-übertriebenen Zeichnung sowie meistens einem kurzen Text (*caption/punchline*), der dem Gezeichneten eine gewisse Perspektive verleiht. Neben der eigentlichen Beschreibung (Was sieht man?) geht es vor allem um die Interpretation (What is the cartoon about?).
Hier sind einige Formulierungen, die dir weiterhelfen könnten:
The author of the cartoon wants to tell us that ...
The cartoon expresses that ...
After having studied the cartoon in detail, I think it is supposed to show ...
On the whole, the cartoon comments on the ...

This symbol gives us some additional information about ...
The eagle symbolises power, but also aggression.
But it could also be interpreted as a symbol of aggression.

The cartoon shows a caricature of the American president.
The features of his face are grossly exaggerated.
The whole depiction (Darstellung) is quite exaggerated.
This makes the president look like a dangerous animal/very aggressive.
This might have a certain purpose. Perhaps the author wants to show us that ...

The punchline consists of a statement saying that ...
The punchline consists of two lines of direct speech. This clearly shows that ...
Of course it is ironic when it says in the punchline that ...
This punchline carries a double meaning.
The caption is not supposed to be taken literally (wortwörtlich).

1 Translate the following sentences into English.

The sentences could be used to describe a political cartoon about Britain and its colonies.

1. Großbritannien wird auf diesem Bild als Löwe dargestellt.
2. Der Löwe ist ein Symbol der Kraft und der Entschlossenheit.
3. Der Cartoon drückt aus, dass Großbritannien seine Kolonien nicht fair behandelte.
4. Die ganze Darstellung ist natürlich sehr übertrieben.
5. Der Text unter dem Bild sollte nicht wörtlich genommen werden.
6. Das soll zeigen, dass die Situation der Einwanderer sehr schwierig ist.

2 Describe the following cartoon.

Start with what you see. Then think about the meaning and write down what the cartoon is about. You can use the words and phrases below.

in the left-hand corner of the cartoon — *to the right* — *next to*

row of animals — *fish-like animal* — *lizard* — *monkey*

symbolises evolution — *millions of years ago*

difference between animals and human beings — *to develop* — *instinct*

food — *search for meaning*

4.5 Personen beschreiben

REMEMBER *Describing a person*

Unter **Personenbeschreibung** ist hier nicht nur die **Beschreibung des Äußeren** (*outward appearance*) zu verstehen, sondern auch die der inneren **Eigenschaften** (*character*) und der **Verhaltensweisen** (*behaviour*). Diese stehen oft im Mittelpunkt der (literarischen) Textanalyse. Aber auch beim Verfassen von Sachtexten musst du oft über Menschen schreiben.

In der Textanalyse unterscheidet man zwischen direkter (expliziter) und indirekter (impliziter) Charakterisierung. (*direct/explicit versus indirect/implicit characterisation*).

Bei der **direkten Charakterisierung** werden Charaktereigenschaften vom Autor direkt genannt.

Beispiel:

He has straight black hair and is an arrogant and selfish man.

Bei der **indirekten Charakterisierung** muss der Leser zwischen den Zeilen lesen, also selbst interpretieren, was gemeint ist.

Beispiel:

When she asked him a question, he didn't even look at her. → He is arrogant.

Du brauchst einen Grundstock von **Adjektiven**, um Personen (und andere Dinge) beschreiben zu können. Eine gute Strategie, Adjektive zu lernen, ist es, sie in Gegensatzpaaren zu lernen. Beispiel: elegant ↔ clumsy/inelegant. Falls dir ein Adjektiv nicht einfällt, beschreibe, was derjenige nicht ist, arbeite also mit dem Gegenteil. Dir fällt z. B. das Wort „tollpatschig" (clumsy) nicht ein. Dann könntest du schreiben: He is not very elegant./He is not exactly elegant.

Die äußere Personenbeschreibung *(outward appearance)*

Bei der Analyse von Abbildungen oder Cartoons, aber auch im Rahmen der Analyse eines Erzähltextes, Theaterstückes oder Films könnte die Beschreibung einer Figur gefordert sein.

Hier sind zunächst wichtige Formulierungen für die äußerliche Beschreibung (*outward appearance*):

He is strong, powerful, healthy, sportive, well-trained, muscular, slim, elegant, good-looking ...

He is weak, skinny, unhealthy, ill, overweight, inelegant, untidy/unkempt (ungepflegt), clumsy, ugly ...

Beispiele:

The **expression of her face** showed that she was really scared of him.

She has an **angry** look on her face.

She looks **worried/puzzled/amazed** ...
She has **blonde/black/brown/curly/straight** hair.
He is **bald**. (hat eine Glatze)
He wears a **moustache/a beard** ...
There is a long **scar** (Narbe) across his left **cheek**. (Wange)
She wears **glasses.**
His teeth are in a very **poor condition.**
Her face is full of **freckles**. (Sommersprossen)
He wears a **brace** (am. Engl.: braces). (Zahnspange)
He has a disability/is **disabled**. (körperlich behindert)
It looks as if he was not too **bright**. (bright heißt hier: klug)
He **sits in a wheelchair.**
He walks on **crutches**.
He has **limped** since he was a boy.
He is **hard of hearing.**
He has been **deaf** (and **dumb**) since birth. (taub/stumm) – Achtung: dumb kann im amerikanischen Englisch auch „dumm" (stupid) bedeuten.
He has a **speech impediment/impairment**. (hat eine Sprachbehinderung)

Hinweis: Achte darauf, dass du bei Behinderungen keine abwertenden Formulierungen wählst.

Charakterisierung einer Person (*characterisation*)
Wenn du den Charakter einer Person darstellen möchtest, brauchst du Formulierungen (meist Adjektive), die die „inneren" Eigenschaften und die Verhaltensweisen einer Person beschreiben. Hier sind ein paar der wichtigsten Formulierungen. Wie schon oben erklärt, ist es sinnvoll, diese Ausdrücke als Gegensatzpaare zu lernen:
The way he speaks to his employees (Angestellte) shows that he is **arrogant**.
His behaviour shows that he is very **modest**. (bescheiden)
This sentence shows that she is very **self-confident**.
He likes to show off all the time. He is a bit of a **show-off.** (angeben/Angeber)
He appears to be rather **self-conscious/insecure.** (unsicher)
Some people lack the **self-confidence** to make contact with others.
He never thinks of others. He is entirely **egoistic**.
He always thinks of others. He is very **considerate**.
This paragraph shows that he is rather **insensitive** towards his wife.
But here the text says that he can also be quite **understanding**.
He is **serious** about everything he does.
They **take** everything very **seriously** indeed.
He acts rather **nervously**.
It looks as if he was quite **relaxed**.

He definitely **wants to make a career**.
He is very **ambitious**. (He shows a lot of ambition.)
They were all quite **easy-going/laid back** about this.
He turned out to be a rather **unpleasant** character.
He is a very **enjoyable** person to be with.
Perhaps he should be more **outgoing**, and not so **shy** and **reserved**.
He is a **sensitive** boy. (sensibel)
She is a **sensible** girl. (vernünftig)
They are **proud** of their children.
He is **jealous** of his sister.
He showed a lot of **responsibility** in this situation.
He acted in a **childish** and **selfish** way.

Tipp: Die folgenden Aufgaben enthalten viele weitere nützliche Formulierungen. Schreibe sie in dein Vokabelheft (oder in deinen Vokabelordner) und lerne sie.

1 Translate the following sentences into German.

1. I don't really like him. He is just too ambitious and selfish. No wonder he is the least popular boy in the class.
2. In the story the woman is depicted as being rather shy and withdrawn. Perhaps that is because she lacks the self-confidence to make the first move.
3. This boy is acting in such a childish way. He simply is not sensible enough to wear his helmet. One day he will end up in a wheelchair.
4. His behaviour towards his father was disgraceful. I think he should show more respect and be more sensitive.
5. When they won the competition they did not show off at all. On the contrary, they were very modest about it.

2 **Translate the following sentences into English.**

1. Sie scheint ein vernünftiges Kind zu sein.
2. Ihr solltet stolz auf euren Sohn sein.
3. John ist schon seit Jahren eifersüchtig auf James.
4. Ich finde, er ist ein sehr unangenehmer Mensch.
5. Sue findet, dass er ein bisschen zu ehrgeizig ist.
6. Ihr solltet euch ein bisschen entspannen.
7. Ihr nehmt wirklich alles viel zu ernst.
8. Versuche, selbstbewusster zu sein.
9. Er hatte noch nie einen so unsicheren Menschen gesehen.
10. Es stellte sich heraus, dass er ein sehr angenehmer Mensch war.

3 **Find the right word.**

Put in a suitable word that goes with the situation. Sometimes there is more than one solution.

1. Your sister has won the national gymnastics championships. You think that's great. You are very ______ ______ her.
2. Karen always wants to be the best. She is very ______.
3. He never knows what to do. He is very ______.
4. They only think of themselves and they don't want to share things with others. They are ______.
5. She keeps herself to herself and does not really want to get into contact with others. She is ______.

4 **Find the opposite of the following expressions.**

(Sometimes there is more than one solution.)

1. hard-working ↔ ______
2. clumsy ↔ ______
3. self-confident ↔ ______
4. sensible ↔ ______
5. considerate ↔ ______
6. introverted ↔ ______
7. dangerous ↔ ______
8. pleasant ↔ ______
9. serious ↔ ______
10. sensitive ↔ ______
11. responsible ↔ ______
12. mature ↔ ______
13. sociable ↔ ______
14. determined ↔ ______

5 Describe the outward appearance of the man in the photograph.

Write down general information first (e.g. his age, the shape and expression of his face). Then describe his face in detail from top (hair) to bottom (neck). You can use the following words and phrases.

oval *straight* *small* *frowning* *forehead* *sweat*

eyebrows *staring* *wide* *upper front teeth even*

lower front teeth are askew *clean-shaven* *no beard*

4.6 Textarbeit/Textanalyse

REMEMBER *Working with texts*

Hinsichtlich der Bearbeitung von Texten gibt es eine Vielzahl von Aufgabenstellungen. Die wichtigsten sind die Zusammenfassung eines Textes oder von Textabschnitten sowie Fragen nach Details, z. B. Why doesn't John talk to his parents?

Eine Zusammenfassung schreiben (*writing a summary*)
Bei einer Zusammenfassung wird von dir eine sachliche Wiedergabe eines Textes erwartet, d.h., du musst den Text möglichst „objektiv" wiedergeben. Dazu gehört die Nennung der **Quelle** (Autor, Jahr, Woher?) sowie die Beantwortung der **typischen W-Fragen** soweit möglich. Meinungsäußerungen deinerseits oder zusätzliche Informationen sind daher nicht erwünscht bzw. entsprechen nicht der Aufgabenstellung.
Der Umfang einer Zusammenfassung beträgt ungefähr ein Viertel bis ein Drittel des Ausgangstextes. Zusammenfassungen werden im Präsens (*present tense*) geschrieben. Es gibt keine direkte Rede und es wird nicht zitiert.

Fragen zum Text (*questions on the text*)
Erwartet wird, dass du Fragen zum Text in vollständigen Sätzen beantwortest. Dabei können, je nach Umfang der Frage, kleine Texte entstehen. Diese sollten dann in sich logisch und sprachlich ansprechend gestaltet werden. Benutze soweit es geht deine eigenen Worte bzw. schreibe nicht aus dem Text ab.

Die folgenden Ausdrücke sind für die Textarbeit wichtig. Lerne sie.

- **There are different kinds of texts:**
  article, report, fairy tale (Märchen), tale (Sage), short story (Kurzgeschichte), novel (Roman), novella (Novelle), play (Theaterstück), radio play (Hörspiel)

- **Important words and expressions for analysing a text are:**
  author (Autor), narrator (Erzähler) – Achtung: Autor und Erzähler einer Geschichte sind nicht identisch und müssen daher auseinandergehalten werden.
  paragraph (Abschnitt), line (Zeile)
  contents of the article (Inhalt)
  source (Quelle)
  setting (Schauplatz, also wo und wann etwas spielt)
  Beispiel: The story is set in New York. → Die Geschichte spielt in New York.
  the intention of the author (die Absicht des Autors)

Hier findest du **Beispielsätze** mit nützlichen Wendungen für die Textarbeit:

- **Source – Where from?**
  The article/story **is from a/taken from** a newspaper.

The story **was written by** Stephen King.
The novel **was written in** 1956.

- **contents** (Inhalt) – **What about?**
  The text **is about** a young boy who ...
  The article **deals with** the growing problem of child poverty.
  The book **depicts** life in the 18th century. (schildert/beschreibt)
  The **theme of** the film is the generation conflict in the royal family.
  The **author says** that Britain is a very rich country. (nicht: tells)
  The writer **tells us**/the reader that we should take greater care of the environment.
  In line 23 it says that nuclear power is quite dangerous. (... steht ...)

- **Setting** (Ort und Zeit des Geschehens) – **When and where?**
  The **story is set** in 19th century London.
  The **play takes place** in the 1990s.

- **Plot** (Handlung) – **What?**
  The **plot** of the story **is as follows:** (Die Handlung ist wie folgt:)
  This is the **storyline** of my favourite film: ...
  The **article describes** the series of events that led up to the murder of Martin Luther King.
  The **events described** in the story take place in New York.

- **Characters** (Figuren) – **Who?**
  The **main character** of the story is a young girl called Sue.
  His **outward appearance** shows that he is a superb athlete and very strong.
  However, **his behaviour** suggests that he is not very good at school.
  The **language he uses** could indicate that his mother tongue is not English.

- **Language/intention of the author** (Sprache und Absicht der Autorin/des Autors) – **How?**
  The **language used** by the author creates a rather threatening atmosphere.
  This **expression shows** that Harry doesn't really like his sister at all.
  The **tense atmosphere is emphasized** by the use of dreamlike images, such as the two children sitting on a cloud.
  By **repeating the same phrase** all over again, the poet wants to emphasize that the old man is indeed very lonely.
  Although the **author does not tell us directly**, it is obvious that he does not agree with the President.
  You can **read between the lines** that the author does not like the idea.

Maybe this is an **allusion** to the fact that she is very adventurous. (Anspielung)
I think the author wants **to convey** the message that all men are equal.
This shows that the writer of the text wants to make the reader think about this problem.
The **solution suggested** by the author is that we should all use less energy in order to protect the environment.
He **concludes** that the rain forest is in great danger and that the world community should act now.

1 **Find a phrase from the above examples which either means the same or is very similar.**

EXAMPLE

In the text it says indirectly that... → dt.: zwischen den Zeilen lesen
In the text you can *read between the lines* that ...

1. He wants to get across the idea that ... → dt.: ausdrücken/herüberbringen
   He wants to ______
2. The story takes place in the Australian outback. → dt.: spielt in
   The story ______
3. What happened in the story shows how he became very rich. → dt.: Ereignisse
   The ______ in the story ...
4. The author stresses the point that ... → dt.: betont
   The author ______ the point that ...
5. At the end of the article he suggests that everybody should ... → dt.: schlussfolgert
   He ______ that everybody should ...

2 **Translate the following expressions into English.**

1. Ein Roman von George Orwell
2. Im Text steht, dass ...
3. Die Geschichte spielt in ...
4. Der Autor sagt, dass ...
5. ... einer Zeitung entnommen

4.7 Stellung beziehen

GOOD TO KNOW *Voicing an opinion*

In vielen Aufgaben, z. B. bei der *composition* oder beim *comment*, aber auch im Unterrichtsgespräch, z. B. während einer Diskussion oder Debatte, wird von dir verlangt, dass du Stellung zu einem Problem beziehst bzw. deine eigene Meinung äußerst.
Die folgenden Formulierungen helfen dir, deine Meinung angemessen auszudrücken, und sind sowohl im Schriftlichen als auch im Mündlichen zu gebrauchen.

- The author may be right **in this point**, but **on the other hand** there are also arguments speaking against him.
- I **don't agree** with that at all.
- I strongly **disagree**.
- I completely agree with this and I **would like to add** that there is even more evidence to support his point of view.
- **Statistics show** that more than 50 per cent of all school leavers don't know what they want to do as a career.
- **Experts claim** (behaupten) that most people don't know enough about this topic.
- I still **strongly believe** that it is better for children to grow up in an intact family.
- **It is obvious**, therefore, that we should introduce new teaching methods.
- **I am convinced that** this would improve the situation.

1 **Translate the following sentences into English.**

1. Ich stimme dem überhaupt nicht zu.
2. Da hast du recht.
3. Meiner Meinung nach gibt es keine Argumente, die das unterstützen.
4. Die Statistiken zeigen, dass sich die Situation verbessert hat.
5. Aus meiner Sicht würde dies keinen Sinn ergeben.

2 **Replace the underlined phrases with a similar expression.**

1. The situation has got better: ______
2. Experts are quite sure that the situation has worsened: ______
3. I don't think you are right: I ______
4. The facts show that I am right: ______
5. I strongly believe that this is a good idea: ______

4.8 Sprachmittlung/Mediation

REMEMBER Mediation

Die Mediation ist eine Übertragung (Sprachmittlung), aber keine Übersetzung eines Textes von der einen in die andere Sprache. In der Regel wird verlangt, dass du einen deutschen Text auf Englisch zusammenfasst. Es geht aber auch umgekehrt, also vom Englischen ins Deutsche. (Letzteres wird später in deinem Leben sicher häufiger von dir erwartet werden.)

Tipp: Da eine Mediation keine Übersetzung ist, entfällt das wortwörtliche Übertragen von Sätzen. Der Vorteil ist, dass du komplizierte Sätze und Formulierungen im Ausgangstext entsprechend vereinfachen kannst, ja sogar oft vereinfachen musst. Das Motto lautet: Simplify your life – keep it simple. Schreibe einfaches, aber korrektes und nachvollziehbares Englisch.

1 Summarize the text in English.

An American exchange student has discovered the following article in your school magazine. He wants to know what the article is about.

Putzen, Betteln und Bibbern: Unsere Straßenkinder in Aktion

Am 19. November engagierten sich die Schülerinnen und Schüler der Klasse 6c für die Straßenkinder dieser Welt, indem sie die Hilfsorganisation „Terre des Hommes“ bei der Aktion „Straßenkinder für einen Tag“ unterstützten. Dafür putzten sie in der Innenstadt Schuhe, verkauften selbstgebastelten Schmuck, campierten in Pappkartons oder bettelten um eine Spende. Dabei sammelten die Kinder höchst interessante Erfahrungen: Das Spektrum der Reaktionen reichte von feindseliger Ablehnung über frappierende Gleichgültigkeit bis zu ganz großer Hilfsbereitschaft.

Das Interesse der Medien war groß, so wurden unsere Schülerinnen und Schüler nicht nur von vielen Zeitungen interviewt, sondern auch vom KIKA mit einem „Platz für Helden“ ausgezeichnet.

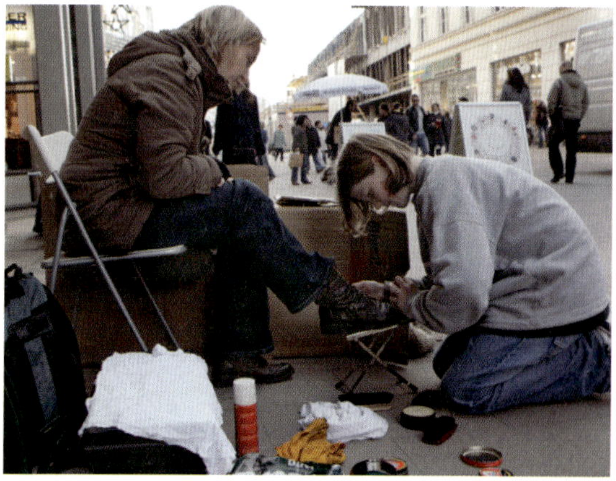

4.9 Übersetzung

REMEMBER *Translation*

Die Übersetzung verlangt eine möglichst genaue Übertragung eines Textes in eine andere Sprache. Das heißt, du solltest so eng wie möglich an dem Originaltext bleiben. Andererseits wird von dir verlangt, dass sich deine Übersetzung auch gut liest, also in ein „gutes Deutsch“ übertragen wird. Solltest du vom Deutschen ins Englische übersetzen, gilt das Gleiche für deinen englischen Text.

Wenn du also merkst, dass eine wörtliche Übersetzung keinen Sinn ergibt, musst du entsprechend frei übersetzen, ganz nach dem folgenden Merksatz:
Übersetze so nah wie möglich, so frei wie nötig. Die Satzstellung ist oft anders, ebenso der Gebrauch der Zeiten. Oft kannst du nicht wörtlich übersetzen, sondern musst eine Entsprechung im Deutschen suchen. Dann ist die Kernfrage:
Was würden wir hier sagen?

Übung macht den Meister. Zur Übung kannst du zusätzlich einige Texte dieses Buches übersetzen.

Vorgehensweise (Schreibplan) bei einer längeren Übersetzung:

1. Text lesen und sich einen Überblick verschaffen. Worum geht es?
2. Schwierige Wörter bzw. Formulierungen oder ganze Sätze unterstreichen.
3. Eine Rohübersetzung (*rough translation*) anfertigen: Den Text im Groben erstellen. Eventuell bei ganz kniffligen Stellen Lücken lassen. Bei Zweifelsfällen Alternativen, also mehrere Lösungsmöglichkeiten, aufschreiben.
4. Eventuell über Änderungen in der Interpunktion nachdenken: Wenn zum Beispiel ein Ausgangssatz sehr kompliziert ist bzw. in der Übersetzung unübersichtlich wird, dann ist es sinnvoll (und erlaubt) den Satz in zwei Sätze aufzuteilen.
5. Nachschlagen von unbekannten Wörtern, prüfen, welche Alternativen die besten sind, prüfen, ob sich der ganze Text flüssig liest, inhaltlich Sinn ergibt und in korrektem Deutsch geschrieben ist. Dazu kannst du dir (oder noch besser einem Partner) deine Übersetzung unter der Fragestellung laut vorlesen: Ergibt das alles Sinn?
6. Anfertigung der Endfassung.

Achtung: ***False friends*** **(Falsche Freunde)**
Nimm dich vor „falschen Freunden“ in Acht *(Beware of false friends.)*. Manche englischen Wörter sehen einem deutschen Wort sehr ähnlich, bedeuten aber etwas ganz anderes. Wenn man diese Wörter falsch verwendet, kommt es oft zu verwirrenden Missverständnissen.

Im Folgenden werden die geläufigsten *false friends* sowie typische andere ***trouble spots*** behandelt, die bei Übersetzungen immer Schwierigkeiten bereiten.

1 Find the right words.

Viele dieser Wörter kennst du sicher, finde die Bedeutung der unbekannten Wörter mithilfe eines Wörterbuchs heraus.

EXAMPLE

decent anständig ⟷ discreet *dezent*

1. actual ______ ⟷ current ______
2. become ______ ⟷ get/receive/obtain ______
3. to blame ______ ⟷ to embarrass s.o. ______
4. desert ______ ⟷ dessert ______
5. brave ______ ⟷ good, well-behaved ______
6. critic ______ ⟷ critique ______
7. famous ______ ⟷ great, splendid ______
8. dome ______ ⟷ cathedral ______
9. genial ______ ⟷ brilliant ______
10. gift ______ ⟷ poison ______
11. hard ______ ⟷ hardly ______
12. novel ______ ⟷ Roman ______
13. map ______ ⟷ briefcase ______
14. floor ______ ⟷ corridor ______
15. murder ______ ⟷ murderer ______
16. note ______ ⟷ grade, mark ______
17. physician ______ ⟷ physicist ______
18. pregnant ______ ⟷ precise, accurate ______
19. preservative ______ ⟷ condom ______
20. rent ______ ⟷ pension ______
21. sensible ______ ⟷ sensitive ______
22. undertaker ______ ⟷ entrepreneur ______

2 Translate the following sentences into German.

1. She has always wanted to become an undertaker.
2. The actual problem is that ...
3. They spend a lot of money on charity.
4. He gave me a gift.
5. That was an interesting lecture.
6. It was a strange fabric.
7. We went to see the dome.
8. Did you hear the critic?
9. You look tired. Come on, take a rest.

10. He <u>overheard</u> the conversation.
11. He got a good <u>rent</u>.
12. Where are the <u>preservatives</u>?
13. This boy <u>blamed me</u> in front of the whole class.

REMEMBER **Feststehende Ausdrücke *(set phrases)***

Folgende Ausdrücke können nicht eins zu eins übersetzt werden. Du musst nach einer entsprechenden deutschen Lösung suchen.

Beispiele:

They became, **as it were**, good friends. → Sie wurden sozusagen gute Freunde.
They became good friends **so to speak**.

above all	=	vor allem
all in all	=	alles in allem
a.m./p.m.	=	vormittags/nachmittags
after all	=	schließlich/immerhin
as for me	=	was mich betrifft
(not) at all	=	überhaupt (nicht)
at the expense of	=	auf Kosten von
by and large/on the whole	=	im Großen und Ganzen
by chance	=	zufällig
by heart	=	auswendig
by the way	=	übrigens
in fact/indeed	=	in der Tat/tatsächlich
in general/generally speaking	=	im Allgemeinen
in vain	=	vergeblich
let alone	=	ganz zu schweigen von/geschweige denn
such as	=	wie (zum Beispiel)
the other day	=	neulich, vor Kurzem
what about	=	was ist mit, wie wäre es mit

3 Translate the following sentences into German.

1. They tried hard to score a goal, but in vain.
2. I met a good friend of his the other day.
3. As for him, he had a difficult time in New York.
4. I'm sorry, but you have to learn your part by heart.
5. He came home rather late, by the way.

GOOD TO KNOW **Deutsches Adverb statt englisches Verb**

Manchmal können bestimmte Verben in englischen Wendungen im Deutschen nur durch Adverbien wiedergegeben werden.

Beispiele:

My dad **is likely** to lose his job.
→ Mein Vater wird wahrscheinlich seine Arbeit verlieren.

She **happened to be** my long lost sister.
→ Sie war zufällig meine seit langem vermisste Schwester.

They **were very fond of** going to football matches.
→ Sie gingen sehr gern zu Fußballspielen.

He always **liked to** flirt with the waitresses.
→ Er flirtete immer gern mit den Kellerinnen.

She **went on/kept on** talking.
→ Sie redete immer weiter.

In the good old days we **used to** play football in the streets.
→ In der guten alten Zeit spielten wir immer Fußball auf der Straße.

4 Translate the following sentences into German.

1. My father likes to go fishing in the morning.
2. This boy happens to be my brother. So leave him alone.
3. She was very fond of hiking in the Rocky Mountains.
4. She is a great dancer. She is likely to have a great career in London.
5. I used to go shopping in the most expensive shops.

GOOD TO KNOW **Nebensatz statt Infinitiv-Konstruktion**

Das Englische verfügt mit Infinitivkonstruktionen sowie Partizipialsätzen und dem Gerundium über Möglichkeiten, Sätze straff zusammenzuziehen. Im Deutschen werden diese Konstruktionen in der Regel mit Nebensätzen übersetzt.

Infinitiv-Konstrukionen (*infinitive constructions*)

Beispiele:

They were the last **to be hired** and the first **to be fired**.
→ Sie waren die letzten, die angestellt wurden, und die ersten, die gefeuert wurden.

He didn't know **what to say**, and she didn't know **what to do**.
→ Er wusste nicht, was er sagen sollte, und sie wusste nicht, was sie tun sollte.
She didn't have **anyone to turn to.**
→ Sie hatte keinen, an den sie sich wenden konnte.
Do you know **how to translate** this sentence?
→ Weißt du, wie man diesen Satz übersetzt?

Gerundien und Partizipien ***(gerunds and participles)***
Beispiele:
Seeing what he had done, he started to cry.
→ Als er sah, was er getan hatte, fing er an zu weinen.
They don't mind sitting out in the sun.
→ Sie haben nichts dagegen, draußen in der Sonne zu sitzen.
Please excuse my being late for the performance, but I couldn't get a taxi.
→ Entschuldigen Sie, dass ich zu spät zur Vorstellung kam, aber ...
I saw my brother drinking lots of beer with his mates.
→ Ich sah, wie mein Bruder sehr viel Bier mit seinen Freunden trank.
He entered the castle holding up his sword.
→ Er betrat das Schloss mit hoch erhobenem Schwert.

5 Translate the following sentences into German.

1. They were the first to be given new passports.
2. Neither of them knew what to do.
3. Do you know how to solve that problem?
4. Seeing who he was, they started waving their hats.
5. They don't mind seeing that film a second time.
6. Please excuse my being late, but I was caught up in a traffic jam.

Test

1 Find the right words.

1. Information, facts and figures: ____ . (The word consists of four letters.)
2. Pie charts or bar charts are: ____________ .
3. If you ask people in the street what they think about a certain issue, you are carrying out a ______ .
4. More than 50 per cent of the population is the ________ .
5. The opposite of number 4 is the ________ .

You get 1 point for each correct answer. **Your points: ___ /5**

2 There is a mistake in each of the following sentences. Correct them.

EXAMPLE

The ~~statistic shows~~ that people tend to eat a lot more fast food than twenty years ago. → *Statistics show*

1. We went to the circus to see the artists performing.
2. I could see my mother on the picture. She was still a child.
3. This painting has quite a frightening affect on me.
4. On the bottom of the picture you can see two girls.
5. At the exhibition we saw a wonderful picture from Titian.

You get 1 point for each correct answer. **Your points: ___ /5**

3 Write down the opposites of the following expressions.

1. He always has to show off, but his brother is very ______ .
2. She is very serious about everything. Her sister is quite ______ .
3. He is so self-conscious. We must teach him to be more ______ .
4. Her brother is still very childish. She, however, is already quite ______ .
5. My mother is outgoing, but my father is rather ______ .

You get 1 point for each correct answer. **Your points: ___ /5**

Besser in

Englisch Lösungsheft

9. Klasse

Gymnasium

Cornelsen SCRIPTOR

1 Revision

Wo offene Aufgabenstellungen eine persönliche Antwort erfordern, wurde auf Lösungsvorschläge weitgehend verzichtet.

Exercise 1 Seite 7

1. Have you ever been to London?
2. Are you reading my book?
3. Didn't you want to help him yesterday?
4. Did you speak to him last week?
5. Will you come to the party tomorrow?

Exercise 2 Seite 7

1. have you?, 2. were they?, 3. didn't we?, 4. didn't you?, 5. have I?

Exercise 3 Seite 7

1. He wanted to know where I had been.
2. He asked (me) how long I would be in London.
3. He asked what I was doing the next day.
4. He wanted to know if I had watched the football match the previous day.
5. He asked (me) to give him my mobile number.

Exercise 4 Seite 8

1. ... to help him with his homework.
2. ... not to tell his parents about Sue.
3. ... to his birthday party.
4. ... asked me to be there at seven.
5. ... told me to hurry up because we were late.

Exercise 5 Seite 9

1. They didn't come to the party.
2. He doesn't like ice-cream.
3. Don't do it now.
4. You don't have to/needn't do your homework today. (must not = nicht dürfen!)
5. This machine has not always/has never worked.

Exercise 6 Seite 9

1. is doing, 2. is repairing, am not, can't, 3. don't think, repaired, is taking, 4. has painted, started, painted, finished, was not, was painting, started, had to, 5. is, 6. will cut/am going to cut, 7. has Mr Anderson been living, 8. moved, has been living

Exercise 7 Seite 12

1. don't get, 2. is, 3. take, 4. would take, 5. could get, 6. won, 7. would have been, 8. would have worked, 9. would have visited

Exercise 8 Seite 12

Lösungsvorschlag:

1. ... we wouldn't have missed the train.
2. ... you take your medicine.
3. ... you brought it back.
4. ... hadn't given us a lift.

Exercise 9 Seite 14

1. We don't have to/needn't start yet.
2. I feel sick. I shouldn't have eaten those three hamburgers.
3. It might have been better if we had stayed at home.
4. I mustn't forget to ask him.

5. Yesterday we were allowed to watch TV until 11 p.m.

Exercise 10 Seite 14

1. was taken, 2. was cancelled, 3. has been repaired, 4. must have been stolen, 5. was opened

Exercise 11 Seite 15

1. He is extremely well qualified for this job.
2. That tastes good.
3. They work hard. (hardly = kaum)
4. She looks nice.
5. He sang beautifully.
6. She can run fast/quickly.
7. We travel to Berlin once a year.
8. He always wears a baseball cap.
9. We fly to London at 4 a.m.

2 Sprache verstehen

2.1 *Modality and Politeness*

Exercise 1 Seite 17

1. In our house everybody has to/should do something.
2. Please take out the rubbish every day.
3. Please be home before 10 p.m.

2.2 *Tenses*

Expressing the future

Exercise 1 Seite 18

1. will have
2. am going to write
3. am going to get it fixed
4. will lend
5. is going to decorate – will help
6. are going to be/will be
7. are going to run out – are we going to/ shall we do
8. is going to be

Exercise 2 Seite 19

1. I'm going to the cinema tonight.
2. The concert begins at 8 o'clock.
3. When does the bus leave?
4. Let's go. Are you coming?
5. What are you doing this Friday?
6. The new maths class starts next week.

Exercise 3 Seite 20

1. am going to, 2. are you doing – are going – Will you come along?, 3. will ask – will do – are – will be, 4. are you going to – leaves – takes/ will take

Simple present or present progressive?

Exercise 4 Seite 21

1. do you want, 2. doesn't love me, 3. is she staring – I don't know, 4. are being, 5. need, 6. don't/can't remember

Simple past or past progressive?

Exercise 5 Seite 22

was doing, heard, listened, was, was coming, felt, picked up, dialled, entered, saw, was snoring, was playing

Present perfect: simple and progessive

Exercise 6 Seite 23

1. has taken, 2. has been cycling, 3. has been living, 4. have you been writing, 5. have you written, 6. have invited, 7. have been watching, 8. has been making – has made

Present perfect or simple past?

Exercise 7 Seite 24

1. Wrong: Dad, did you play a lot of football when you were young?
2. Correct
3. Wrong: Where were you yesterday?

4. Wrong: We are looking for Martin. Have you seen him?
5. Correct
6. Wrong: When did he find out that his boss has been having an affair with his wife?
7. Correct

Past perfect: simple and progessive

Exercise 8 Seite 25

1. went, 2. had never played, 3. broke down,
4. had been playing, 5. had been following,
6. was having, 7. had not planned,
8. was – had been waiting

Participles

Exercise 9 Seite 26

1. Having seen the film three times already, I really didn't want to see it again.
2. Not knowing what to do, he closed the door and pretended he wasn't there.
3. They found him lying on the ground seriously injured.
4. Caught in the act, he finally had to admit that he did it.
5. She owns an amazing guitar once played by Jimi Hendrix.
6. Covered in snow, the mountains were a fantastic sight.

Exercise 10 Seite 26

1. Ich möchte so nicht behandelt werden.
2. Gemütlich im Bett liegend begann er von einem wunderschönen Tag zu träumen.
3. Die mehr als 5 Millionen Mal verkaufte Hitsingle machte ihn zu einem reichen Mann.
4. Ich sah, wie sie wieder dieses fantastische Kleid trug.
5. Dave hörte, wie jemand an der Tür klopfte.

2.3 *Gerund and infinitive*

Exercise 1 Seite 28

1. to turn up, 2. being/to be, 3. finishing,
4. to go out, 5. to drive, 6. not to give, 7. flying,
8. travelling, 9. writing, 10. finding out, 11. seeing,
12. to talk, 13. visiting, 14. looking, 15. to pass

Exercise 2 Seite 29

1. a. Bitte vergiss nicht, den Einkauf zu machen.
   b. Ich erinnere mich, den Einkauf an diesem Tag gemacht zu haben.
2. a. Er hielt an, um eine Zigarette zu rauchen.
   b. Er hörte mit dem Rauchen von Zigaretten auf.
3. a. Hat er wirklich vergessen, dir von der Party zu erzählen?
   b. Er wird nie vergessen, wie er sie zum ersten Mal sah.

2.4 *Position of adverbs*

Exercise 1 Seite 30

1. He did his homework quickly.
2. She also lost her dinner money.
3. Do you play the guitar every day?
4. Correct
5. Don't go to bed so late.
6. I can never remember her name.
7. Correct
8. She usually has a lot of homework to do.
9. They will never be my friends.
10. We should never have eaten this.
11. Correct
12. I go to my friend's house every morning.

Exercise 2 Seite 31

1. I would like you to stop smoking.
2. He needs money to buy a ticket.
3. She went into hospital for an operation.
4. Has he got enough bodyguards to protect him?
5. Is this a special device for cleaning the car?
6. I'm sorry to hear that he has left the school.

2.5 *Defining and non-defining relative clauses*

Exercise 1 Seite 32

1. The CD I have just listened to is by Metallica.
2. The Beatles, who were a famous pop group, split up in the early seventies.
3. Sherlock Holmes, who was a very intelligent man, solved many difficult cases.
4. The car which he wanted to sell to us had in fact been stolen the night before.

5. The men who were arrested the day before yesterday are responsible for three attacks on British troops. The other men were not connected with the crime.
6. The gun that was used in the murder was found in a nearby river.
7. The prime suspect, who was living in Paris at the time, was Trevor Sams.
8. The police officer who was carrying an infrared camera was positioned on the roof, whilst the other one watched the road from a car parked opposite the house.

2.6 *Conditional clauses*

Exercise 1 Seite 34

1. If it rains on Saturday, I won't need to water the plants.
2. If she had known that her parents were coming, she would have prepared something to eat.
3. If they were interested in the house, they would look at it.
4. We would have called you if we had known you were in town.
5. If you had practised the piano when you were young, you wouldn't regret it now.
6. If you give me your address, I'll visit you.

Exercise 2 Seite 34

1. If he had missed the train, he wouldn't have got the job.
2. My mother is going to make her famous apple pie if/when my uncle comes on Sunday.
3. I would be delighted if our team won the match tomorrow.

2.7 *The passive*

Exercise 1 Seite 35

1. He was given the keys, so he let himself in.
2. He was not invited to the party.
3. How much will I get paid for the job?
4. When we arrived at the airport we found that our flight had been cancelled.
5. This is a serious problem. Something must be done about it now.

Exercise 2 Seite 36

1. He was forced to hand over the money.
2. They were shown around.
3. They were told where to sleep.
4. She will be taken to hospital.
5. We could be taught by my aunt.

2.8 *Reported speech*

Exercise 1 Seite 36

1. Do you know where the toilet is?
2. He wanted to know if/whether I knew him.
3. She couldn't remember what his name was.
4. We wondered why he hadn't/didn't come.
5. He wanted to know when the show began/would begin.
6. She said (that) she wouldn't come.
7. He told us that they didn't stand a chance.
8. They informed us that it hadn't rained for ages.
9. She complained that she didn't want to live there.
10. They had no idea who the/that child was.

2.9 *Prepositions*

Exercise 1 Seite 39

1. at, 2. of, 3. for, 4. from, 5. by, 6. in, 7. from, 8. on, 9. of, 10. of, 11. on, 12. for, 13. by, 14. of, 15. for, 16. to

Exercise 2 Seite 39

1. The reason for this misunderstanding is that he can't speak English.
2. The novel was written by William Faulkner.
3. That wasn't very clever of you.
4. He is very good at music. Everybody is very impressed with his playing.
5. Were you surprised by this?
6. I think I should go on a diet.
7. They asked me for help.
8. They sent the documents by post.
9. Do you believe in miracles?
10. You can be proud of yourselves.
11. Don't look at me. I'm only looking for my keys.
12. I'm not in today. Can you take care of that?

2.10 *Phrasal verbs*

Exercise 1 Seite 40

1. reduce speed, 2. agree, 3. separated/divorced, 4. cancelled, 5. increase speed, 6. invented, 7. saw, 8. continue, 9. succeeded, 10. managed, 11. avoid

Exercise 2 Seite 41

Hello Everybody,
turned on (begeistert), run down (heruntergekommen), do it up (renovieren), shut down (schließen), put up (zurechtkommen), turned out (sich herausstellen), knocked the price down (Preis runterhandeln), getting along (auskommen), got out of hand (außer Kontrolle geraten), passed out (ohnmächtig werden), throw up (erbrechen), off-putting (abstoßend), cut down (verringern, verkleinern), push off (abhauen), set off (auslösen), went on (weitermachen), told off (deutlich ermahnen), turned out (s. o.), was up against (gegen), felt a bit down (waren niedergeschlagen), came back (wiederkommen), cheer them up (aufmuntern), worked out (funktionieren), got along (s. o.), carry on (weitermachen), turned out (s. o.)
rip off (abzocken), catch up (einholen), got away with it (damit durchkommen)

2.11 *Spelling*

Exercise 1 Seite 42

1. correct, 2. correct, 3. studied, 4. worried, 5. correct, 6. splitting

2.12 *A mixed bag of trouble spots*

Exercise 1 Seite 43

1. Please tell me your name.
2. I told him.
3. Yesterday I had a wonderful dessert.
4. I'd like to become a pilot.
5. That was a difficult task.
6. The box was too heavy for me.
7. I'm going to Switzerland tomorrow.
8. I don't want to go out now.
9. I'd like to have two postcards.
10. Can you make us some tea?
11. The water is boiling.
12. My father likes cooking.
13. Please let me sleep.
14. My weekend was terrible. My parents made me clean the garage.
15. Can you take me to the lake?
16. We've got a house by the sea/at the seaside.
17. He won first prize and got a good grade/mark in physics.
18. He got a good price for his car.
19. I'm interested in technology.
20. His technique is great. He really is a brilliant football player.
21. If you don't go now, there will be trouble/(or:) you'll be in trouble.
22. When I get home I always drink a homemade milkshake.
23. I couldn't do the homework.
24. Stockport is near Manchester.
25. What's your opinion? What do you think?
26. That's wonderful news.
27. The boss is ill today.
    Mr Schmidt, would you please take over?
28. We have overtaken a lot of lorries/trucks today.
29. Have you finished your exercises/tasks?
30. Are you ready?

Exercise 2 Seite 44

1. Sie ist eine ganz normale Frau.
   dt. ordinär: = common
2. Wer ist hier der Koch?
   dt. Chef = boss
3. Willst du den Lastwagen überholen?
   dt. übernehmen = to take over
4. Er war so ein tapferer Junge.
   dt. brav = good/well-behaved
5. Sie machte sich Vorwürfe.
   dt. sich blamieren: to make a fool of oneself
6. Komm, sei vernünftig.
   dt. sensibel = sensitive
7. Ich habe ihr Gespräch belauscht.
   dt. überhören: don't catch/ignore (absichtlich)
8. Kann ich eine Quittung für das Medikament haben?
   dt. ärztliches Rezept = prescription, Kochrezept = recipe

9. Sie war sehr mitfühlend/verständnisvoll, als ich ihr von meinem Problem erzählt habe.
   dt. symphatisch = pleasant, likeable, nice;
   engl. sympathetic = understanding.

Exercise 3 Seite 45

1. She is such a sweet little girl.
2. We had such terrible weather.
3. Have you ever seen such a tall building?
4. How can you/one be so forgetful?
5. I don't like such people.

Exercise 4 Seite 45

1. Ein Bankraub könnte jahrelanges Gefängnis bedeuten, wenn du gefasst wirst.
2. Ich wollte nicht unhöflich sein.
3. Entschuldigung, aber ich weiß nicht, was du meinst/was du sagen willst.
4. Er wollte nicht so spät nach Hause kommen.
5. Nun, was soll das jetzt (bedeuten)?
6. Heißt/Bedeutet das, dass du nicht kommen kannst?
7. Der Gewinn des Pokalfinales gab ihrer Handballkarriere eine neue Bedeutung/eine Wende.
8. Was meinst du damit?/Was willst du damit sagen?
9. Das heißt, wir werden nicht zum Spiel gehen.

Exercise 5 Seite 46

off to __ school, how was __ school, I'll be at the school, __ life is certainly hard, the life of your Dad, at __ work, in the office, go to the toilet, I'm going to __ bed, They went into the church, go to __ church, looking at the church, at the hotel, about __ life during the French Revolution, the life of young people

Exercise 6 Seite 47

1. a teacher, an electrician, __ British Telecom
2. for __ dinner, after __ school, going to the cinema
3. __ life is difficult, look at the life of the big stars, such a good time
4. a really interesting workshop, a Scotsman __ Time went by, the great time I had
5. __ June is my favourite month, the June of 2002, on my way to __ school, to __ Switzerland, the Netherlands, in the summer, at Lake Geneva

Exercise 7 Seite 47

1. She is the most famous woman in the world. Many people say, however, that she can also be the most difficult/complicated one.
2. Tim isn't as fast as Ann but he is better than Ann at basketball.
3. This year is the worst of all. Everything has become more expensive.
4. We are luckier than Jack but not as lucky as my grandmother.
5. He is one of the world's most famous actors but not as popular as his brother.
6. Maths is getting more difficult all the time.
7. Although he was the youngest player, he scored most goals.
8. He is richer than Bill Gates.
9. They are getting more money, but not enough to buy an even bigger house.

Test

Exercise 1 Seite 48

1. present progressive, 2. simple past,
3. present perfect, 4. past perfect,
5. going to-future, 6. past progressive

Exercise 2 Seite 48

1. No. 3, 2. No. 2, 3. No. 5, 4. No. 4, 5. No. 1

Exercise 3 Seite 48

1. at - by, 2. during - at, 3. at, 4. during, 5. at,
6. in - by, 7. in - on, 8. at - to - about - into - of

Exercise 4 Seite 49

1. are going to crash, 2. will give, 3. is,
4. are you doing - Will you join , 5. lived,
6. have you been working, 7. am staying,
8. need, 9. was doing - went - was,
10. had seen - knew - was

Exercise 5 Seite 49

1. I hate coming/being late.
2. I found him practising the guitar.

3. Confused by the great number of people yesterday, he didn't want to perform.
4. Coming from Germany, he was used to cold winters.
5. Looking at the sky he realized that it would soon start raining.

Exercise 6 Seite 50

1. to get, 2. writing, 3. joining, 4. to smoke, 5. smoking

Exercise 7 Seite 50

1. If you don't do it now, we will be in real difficulties.
2. They were given a certificate.
3. I couldn't remember exactly when he was arrested.
4. That's typical of that kind of art.
5. Did you hear her on the radio yesterday?
6. What's the reason for that?
7. They were caught and have to go to prison.
8. I told you so.
9. Sometimes you are such an egoist/so selfish.
10. Life is sometimes hard, especially the life of young people.

Exercise 8 Seite 50

Lösungsvorschlag:

1. Please don't smoke in our kitchen.
2. My mum would like us to go and see Mr Pearson right now.
3. Perhaps you should spend more time on your homework.
4. My dad would like us to be home by ten o'clock.
5. It would be great if you didn't always take my CDs.

Exercise 9 Seite 50

1. good, 2. hard, 3. fast, 4. perfect, 5. perfectly

Exercise 10 Seite 51

1. They went into/entered the bank quickly. *Or:* They quickly went into/entered the bank.
2. Do you go swimming every day?
3. Would you like to play table tennis this evening?
4. He had an accident three years ago.
5. Next year we are going to buy a house in London./We are going to buy a house in London next year.

Exercise 11 Seite 51

1. no commas
2. John, who had just finished high school, got the job.
3. no commas
4. no commas
5. Metallica, who were very successful in the 1990s, are going on tour once more.

Exercise 12 Seite 51

1. If he doesn't come tomorrow, I will talk to his brother.
2. If it hadn't snowed, we would have been on time.
3. I would be glad/happy if I had a bit more time for my hobbies.
4. It wouldn't have been so bad if he had been a bit nicer to us.
5. She will tell him if/when she sees him tomorrow.

Exercise 13 Seite 51

1. ... he didn't know him.
2. ... if/whether I could do her a favour.
3. ... if I would come to the party next evening/on the following evening.
4. ... that she could have known about it.
5. ... if/whether I had ever seen such a big fish.

3.1 Lesen und verstehen

Australia's "Stolen Generations"

Exercise 2 Seite 55

Lösungsvorschlag:

1. The text deals with/is about the so-called "stolen generations" in Australia, aborigine children who were taken away from their parents to be brought up in a white environment.

Exercise 3 Seite 55

1. They thought that many Aborigines were incapable of raising their children properly.
2. The children would receive a better education and grow up in better social conditions. Therefore they would stand a much better chance of having a career.
3. They either lured them into traps or just took them away from their parents.
4. They became aware of it in the late 1990s.
5. They demand financial compensation.
6. In the second-to-last paragraph (l. 27) the author uses the word "imagine" and says that "it must have hurt incredibly" (l. 29). Here, he clearly asks the readers to sympathise with the "stolen generations".

Exercise 4 Seite 55

1. They were supposed to receive a better education. → erhalten/bekommen
2. People got to know about the programme. → gelangte an die Öffentlichkeit/wurde bekannt gemacht
3. They had not realised that there ... → Es war ihnen kaum bewusst, dass ...
4. They are demanding more than just an apology. → Sie verlangen mehr als eine bloße Entschuldigung.
5. So far the government has not reacted/given an answer. → hat nicht reagiert/geantwortet

Exercise 5 Seite 56

1. Es könnte leicht als eine der schändlichsten politischen Maßnahmen in der Geschichte Australiens bezeichnet werden.
2. Man hielt Aborigines für unfähig, ihre Kinder vernünftig/richtig zu erziehen.
3. Die Kinder wurden entweder in Waisenhäuser oder Kinderheime gesteckt oder sie wurden weißen Pflegeeltern übergeben.
4. In anderen Fällen wurden die Kinder einfach mit Gewalt, gegen den Willen ihrer Eltern, aus der Familie genommen.
5. Die Absicht war, dass die Kinder eine bessere Erziehung bekommen sollten und unter sozialen Bedingungen aufwachsen würden, die ihnen einen besseren Start garantierten und eine spätere Karriere ermöglichen würden.
6. Historiker schätzen, dass mindestens 100.000 Kinder von ihren Familien getrennt wurden, bis das Programm schließlich in den späten 1960er-Jahren gestoppt wurde.

Bush flies. A letter from Australia

Exercise 2 Seite 58

Peter → working holiday in Australia, outback, good time, friendly people
Bush flies → real nuisance, drive people crazy
Why so many flies? → colonists/white settlers brought cows to Australia, cow dung as ideal breeding ground → flies multiply
What can be done? (countermeasures) → breeding or importing dung beetles → supposed to eat up cow dung → not very successful yet

Exercise 3 Seite 58

Lösungsvorschlag:

Hi James,
I've just got an interesting e-mail from an old friend of mine, Peter, from down under. He writes that everything would just be fine if it wasn't for the flies, bush flies to be precise. There must be millions of them around, pestering you wherever you are and whatever you do. It must be quite horrible.
Peter writes that the reason why there are so many flies is that the colonists brought cows to Australia in the 19th century. And the cow dung – and there must be a lot of it because there are so many cattle ranches in Australia – provides an

ideal breeding ground for the bush flies. So they multiply like wild.
The Australians have tried to breed dung beetles, or import them from Africa. The beetles were supposed to eat up a great deal of the cow dung, thereby destroying the flies' breeding ground. But (unfortunately for Peter) that hasn't worked out yet. Anyway, I didn't know anything about those flies, did you?
Bye for now,
Rob

Exercise 4 Seite 58

1. False: The bush flies are a nuisance, but are not really dangerous.
2. False: Australian bush flies were already there. The British settlers brought cows to Australia and the cow dung provided an ideal breeding ground for the flies.
3. True
4. Not in the text
5. False. The dung beetle is supposed to eat up the cow dung. Then the bush flies would lose their breeding ground and their numbers would decrease.
6. Not in the text
7. True
8. Not in the text

Exercise 5 Seite 58

1. I had a lot of work to do/I was very busy.
2. It is very irritating./It is quite nerve-racking./ It's driving us mad.
3. .... multiply in great numbers.
4. They seem to be enjoying themselves/to be having a good time.
5. ... from Australia.

Exercise 6 Seite 58

1. They find it very irritating/unpleasant.
   Sie finden es höchst ärgerlich.
2. They really cause a lot of trouble.
   Sie sind ein echtes Ärgernis.
3. They make life very difficult for me.
   Sie machen mir das Leben (äußerst) schwer.
4. The farm is located/situated in a very remote area.
   Die Farm ist mitten im Nirgendwo/in einer sehr abgeschiedenen Gegend.
5. People found that .../It became clear that ...
   Es erwies sich, dass die Fliegen äußerst erfreut über den Kuhmist waren.

A personal report

Exercise 2 Seite 61

1. Introduction: Nehru International School
2. Problems with the electric kettle
3. Using computers at Nehru International
4. Food
5. Transport
6. Negotiating prices (rickshaw fares)
7. Conclusion/greeting

Exercise 3 Seite 61

Lösungsvorschlag:

1. They share a little apartment right in the school building.
2. They have got a computer with Internet access in their room and there are two more computers in the classroom. However, they cannot use them all the time as there are frequent power cuts.
3. There is a McDonald's but it serves more Indian than American food and does not serve beef at all.
4. They like travelling around Delhi by rickshaw scooter (a rickshaw powered by a scooter engine with covered backseat for two passengers).
5. For them, negotiating prices is sometimes difficult as some drivers do not speak English and the girls cannot understand their facial expressions. However, Caroline and Sue have gained some experience by now and take it as a challenge to negotiate reasonable prices.

Exercise 4 Seite 61

Caroline und Susan sind seit ein paar Wochen an der Nehru International School in Neu Delhi, wo sie sich ein Zimmer direkt im Schulgebäude teilen, das sogar über einen Internetanschluss verfügt. Allerdings gibt es immer wieder Stromausfälle, sodass das Arbeiten am Rechner manchmal nicht gerade einfach ist.

Am liebsten erkunden sie die Stadt mit der „scooter rickshaw“, einer motorisierten Rikscha, die über eine gepolsterte Sitzbank verfügt. Dabei scheint dass Verhandeln des Fahrpreises ein Abenteuer für sich zu sein, weil manche Fahrer kein Englisch können und die Mädchen (noch) nicht in der Lage sind, aus deren Gesichtsausdrücken Rückschlüsse zu ziehen. Mittlerweile haben sie aber so viel Verhandlungsgeschick erworben, dass sie sich nicht mehr so leicht übers Ohr hauen lassen.
Insgesamt geht es ihnen gut und sie würden sich über eine Mail von euch riesig freuen.

Exercise 5 Seite 61

1. After a long and tiring walk of about 30 seconds ... (meant ironically: they live in the school building)
2. ... gave up
3. that sometimes you don't know whether they are saying 'yes' or 'no'
4. ... have said that it is true

Children stressed out by ads

Exercise 2 Seite 62

Lösungsvorschlag:

1. Children have become direct targets of advertising campaigns. Watching so many commercials on TV results in constant pressure to dress and look like the models and to have all the latest goods.
2. The consequences are stress, especially on girls, leading to depression and lack of self-esteem because they can't live up to the ideals of fashion and beauty that they see.

Exercise 3 Seite 62

1. False: They have a passive role as they are the consumers, not the producers of adverts.
2. Not in the text
3. Not in the text
4. False: They show the same stress symptoms as adults.
5. True

Exercise 4 Seite 62

1. an essay read by a lot of people/by a wide audience
2. lack of self-confidence
3. with very serious negative consequences

Exercise 5 Seite 62

Lösungsvorschlag:

Kinder leiden unter Werbung
Wissenschaftler haben herausgefunden, dass sich viele Kinder durch die Fernsehwerbung unter Druck gesetzt fühlen, bestimmten Schönheitsidealen zu entsprechen. Dies wirkt sich zum Beispiel auf die Auswahl der Kleidung aus. Besonders Mädchen geraten unter Stress, da sie sich, oft vergeblich, bemühen, den von der Industrie vertretenen Schönheitsidealen zu entsprechen, zum Teil mit schlimmen Folgen.

Test

Exercise 2 Seite 65

1. they go out so much., 2. something that needs to be done., 3. many western-style shops., 4. they are not registered in most travel guides., 5. which are all quite small in size., 6. it difficult to find a shopkeeper who spoke English., 7. functioned all right., 8 there was often something missing., 9. a rather casual language.

Exercise 3 Seite 65

Lösungsvorschlag:

1. a) The western style shops in India are fairly expensive (at least for Caroline and Susan).
   b) There are no western-style supermarkets, such as Wal-Mart.
   c) There are separate markets for different products.
   d) The markets are not named according to what they sell but according to where they are.
   e) For Caroline and Susan it is very difficult to find out where the markets are.
2. The "three-step-dance" describes Caroline's and Susan's efforts to find out where certain markets are. The first step involves looking at travel guides, the second one means e-mailing

acquaintances from Delhi and the third one is calling friends.

3. Das Problem war, dass das Kleidungsstück nicht vollständig war. Zunächst musste sich Susan den passenden Gürtel auf der Straße dazukaufen und dann alles zu einem Schneider auf dem Parkplatz bringen, der schließlich die Ärmel annähte.

3.2 Hören und verstehen

Exercise 2 Seite 67

1. of the same age.; from a similar social class.; you spend your free time with.
2. having a problem with alcohol.; behaving in a very aggressive way.
3. wanting to stay with the group.
4. experiment with new hairstyles.; develop their own way of life.
5. help you get over periods of uncertainty about yourself.; give you some good ideas about morals and values.
6. keeping in close contact with them.
7. in a rather balanced, objective way.

Exercise 3 Seite 68

Lösungsvorschlag:

1. Notes: same age, same group of friends, similar social background
   Answer: It's the group of people of the same age and a similar social background, e.g. your friends.
2. Notes: misbehaving, start smoking, drugs, violence
   Answer: They start misbehaving, take up smoking and get involved in drugs or violence.
3. Notes: part of the group, not stick out, not be different
   Answer: They want to be part of the group/ belong to the group and not be different. So they do what the group does, as they don't want to stick out by saying no.
4. Notes: own ideas, own life style, parents lose control
   Answer: Teenagers suddenly develop their own ideas and lifestyle, and parents think they are losing control over their own children.
5. Notes: ignores parents, spends time with mates
   Answer: She has suddenly started to ignore her parents and spends most of her time with her mates.
6. Notes: positive values: trust, faithfulness, fairness
   Answer: A peer group can provide positive values such as trust, faithfulness and fairness, and help the individual get over periods of uncertainty and questioning about themselves.
7. Notes: support, listen, keep up communication
   Answer: Parents should take their children seriously and support them by listening to their worries. They should keep up communication even if their children behave in a difficult way.

Exercise 4 Seite 68

1. we'll be talking about peer group pressure among young people.
2. is the same age as you are. So the peer group are people about as old as you, who come from a similar social group, for instance your class mates or your friends.
3. smoking, drinking, drug taking or violent behaviour.
4. worry about their sons and daughters getting too close to such groups?
5. who want to develop their own ideas and often create their own lifestyle.
6. and prepared to listen to their kids' ideas, and their worries.

Exercise 5 Seite 69

1. exactly, 2. related to, 3. desire - to belong to,
4. complex, 5. to stick out, 6. adolescent
7. discover

Exercise 6 Seite 69

1. Gruppenzwang. Eltern machen sich Sorgen, wenn ihre Kinder sich einer Gruppe Gleichaltriger anschließen und ihr Verhalten gegenüber den Eltern, aber auch allgemein, ändern.
2. Die Gruppe vermittelt positive Werte und Verhaltensweisen und übt so einen guten Einfluss auf die Jugendlichen aus. Andererseits kann es vorkommen, dass Jugendliche sich negativ ver-

ändern, da sie sich oft dem Gruppenzwang innerhalb ihrer Clique unterwerfen und dann Dinge tun, die sie sonst eher nicht tun würden.
3. Eltern sollten ihre Kinder besonders dann unterstützen, wenn die Situation schwierig ist. Sie sollten also den Kontakt halten und sich ernsthaft für die Sorgen und Nöte ihrer Kinder interessieren.

Smoking teens

Exercise 1 Seite 69

1. She doesn't listen to Carol and walks out on her/leaves the room.
2. She will spend too much money on cigarettes and make the house stink.
3. Why do young people start smoking? What can she do to make her daughter stop smoking?

Exercise 2 Seite 70

1. is a fairly complex issue.
2. not helped very much.
3. Carol stops smoking.

Exercise 3 Seite 70

1. distressed, 2. confronted her with the issue, 3. stink the place out, 4. take up the habit, 5. desperately, 6.making an effort – follow suit

Exercise 4 Seite 70

1. This is Carol Scott.
2. The other night ...
3. Nicotine is extremely addictive.
4. ... although she should know better.
5. ... despite large campaigns from the government.
6. ... to make our children aware of the dangers of smoking.
7. the introduction of quite a few restrictions
8. public place
9. a proven fact
10. making an effort

Staying out late

Exercise 1 Seite 71

1. ... fifteen-year-old boy.
2. ... is doing well.
3. ... his father needn't worry.
4. ... to talk to him.
5. ... what he can do to make him come home earlier.
6. ... an important step to learn to make their own decisions/judgements.
7. ... be prepared to allow him a certain amount of freedom.
8. ... know where his son is and who he is with, and to make acceptable rules.

Exercise 2 Seite 71

1. rather, 2. to make your own judgements, 3. have every right to, 4. reach(ing) a reasonable agreement, 5. in case of an emergency

Exercise 3 Seite 71

1. doing all right at school
7. no simple solution to this
6. at a reasonable hour
11. reasonable agreement
9. be prepared to
8. staying out late
10. certain amount of freedom
5. find it hard to talk to him
4. no need to worry
2. come home rather late
12. set rules
3. quite honestly

Exercise 4 Seite 71

1. He's doing all right at school.
2. I'm afraid there is no simple solution to this.
3. So you should be prepared to allow your son a certain amount of freedom.
4. ... then you can reach a fair compromise.

Friendships

Exercise 1 Seite 72

Lösungsvorschlag:

1. She is worried about her daughter hanging out with the wrong kind of people.
2. Boys tend to have several friends they can do activities with. Girls find it more important to have one "best friend".

3. Young people learn to get along with people, to develop social skills and to build up relationships.
4. In general, she should trust her daughter. But if the daughter gets involved in any criminal activities she must do something about it, put her foot down and stop it.

Exercise 2 Seite 72

... that friendships play a vital role in young people's ability to develop social skills and build up relationships. A lot of this is about experimenting and finding out who you are and what kind of people you can get along and feel comfortable with.

Exercise 3 Seite 72

1. has been hanging around with ..., 2. ... a great deal older, 3. I worry myself sick, 4. develops into, 5. share, 6. if something fishy is going on, 7. you must put your foot down

Teenagers at war (part one)

Exercise 1 Seite 72

1. discovered child soldiers as a good topic for selling their products. - introduced the world to a new problem of children at war.
2. there are indeed a lot of dramatic reports on child soldiers. - the situation of child soldiers in some African countries has worsened.
3. throughout human history.
4. easy to control. - very radical. - do as they are told.
5. criminals. - warlords.
6. economic interests.
7. do not care about the situation. - are not really in control of their territory.

Exercise 2 Seite 73

1. ... about a rather sad and frightening topic.
2. ... is it only that the media have just discovered that reports on that issue sell well?
3. ... sense of sensationalist reporting on this topic.
4. ... has reached a new dimension with more and more teenagers being involved.

Exercise 3 Seite 73

1. issue - being involved, 2. misused,
3. collapsed - hesitate, 4. on the whole, does it make any sense to use

Teenagers at war (part two)

Exercise 1 Seite 74

Lösungsvorschläge:

1. Notes: poverty, mass unemployment, lack of education, hopelessness, no future
   Answer: Many African countries face a very high rate of poverty and unemployment. Due to the lack of education, many young people have no hope and don't see a future for themselves.
2. Notes: no control, breakdown of law and order, warlords replace politicians/state
   Answer: Governments are not really in control of their territories because they don't have the money to pay for an efficient army or police force. So they can't keep up law and order, and as a consequence the warlords take over in certain parts of the country, replacing political leaders and the state.
3. Notes: children persuaded to join, financial gain, abducted, fear of being murdered
   Answer: Children are either talked into joining a private army, with leaders promising them a lot of money, or they are simply abducted (taken away) from their parents' homes. The parents can't do much about this, because if they intervene, they risk being murdered.
4. Notes: spirits on their side, protection by magic (spells), children not afraid
   Answer: Leaders often manage to convince children that the spirits are on their side and will protect them. Furthermore, as many Africans still believe in magic, they tell the children that they are protected by magic charms and that nothing can happen to them in battle. So the children feel quite safe and act fearlessly.
5. Notes: international awareness, aid programmes, homes, orphanages, keep them off the streets
   Answer: The international community has become aware of the problem and has started aid programmes to improve the situation.

These have helped build homes and orphanages for homeless children to give them something to do and keep them off the streets and out of the hands of the warlords.

Exercise 2 Seite 74

1. get out of hand
2. mass unemployment, lack of education, hopelessness
3. keep up law and order
4. local warlords have replaced the political leaders
5. earn a fortune
6. ... that they would be better off than their parents
7. protected by magic charms
8. homes and orphanages are being built
9. end up in the streets
10. definitely not enough to solve the problem

Exercise 3 Seite 74

child soldiers, current political and economic situation, lost its authority, the fight over resources, recognize what they would be drawn into, would not join such a group

Test

Deborah Shurer on German-American stereotypes

Exercise 1 Seite 75

1. Americans on Germany:
   orderly country
   clean
   Autobahn, fast cars
   soccer violence
   punctuality: trains are on time
   Germans on America:
   nice people, but superficial
   people pretend friendliness, don't mean it
   fast food: hamburgers, French fries
   fat people
2. Road rage is loss of self control because of traffic or driving incidents.
3. A car that uses up a lot of gas (British English: petrol).
4. Americans on Germany:
   a) Not every German plays football or cares for it.
   b) German trains are not always on time.
   Germans on America:
   a) There are also school-shootings in Germany, not only in America
   b) Not every American has got a big car, as these are not so popular anymore.
5. Sales of SUVs have gone down because they use up so much gas. And as the price for gas has risen dramatically over the last two years, many people cannot afford it anymore.

Exercise 2 Seite 75

3. what you might expect
4. sausage and sauerkraut
5. stuff like that
6. impressed with
7. will probably know about soccer
8. some of the stereotypes
9. encountered
10. very nice, but superficial
11. they ... won't really mean it
12. in terms of food

Exercise 3 Seite 76

1. differences, 2. orderly, 3. well-informed, 4. frequent, 5. plenty of, 6. gone up

Exercise 4 Seite 76

1. about
2. what is a typical American and what is a typical German
3. I have lived twenty years of my life in Germany and about twenty years in the U.S.
4. what you might expect
5. is a very orderly country
6. impressed
7. trains are on time
8. like the Autobahn
9. impressed with
10. drive as fast as you want to anywhere on the Autobahn
11. really true
12. well-informed
13. know about soccer

14. some of the stereotypes
15. direction
16. probably encountered
17. superficial
18. invite you to their houses
19. won't really mean it
20. want to be friends
21. when you call them
22. don't really want to
23. in terms of food
24. associate
25. French fries
26. leads to
27. which in my experience
28. really fat
29. so fat they need big cars
30. matter of violence
31. violent society
32. school shootings
33. National Rifle Association
34. I don't know if you've
35. road rage
36. mad about traffic
37. pull their guns and shoot each other
38. frequent
39. I really don't believe in
40. plenty of people
41. couldn't care less
42. the trains are not always on time
43. school shootings
44. big cars are no longer that popular
45. gas prices have gone up
46. sold as much
47. gas guzzlers
48. burn so much gas
49. watch out
50. that much money
51. afford to buy the car
52. afford to use it
53. afford the gas on a regular basis

4 Texte schreiben

4.1 Briefe verfassen

Exercise 1 Seite 80

Lösungsvorschlag mit Erläuterungen (Die Ziffern im Brief verweisen auf die Erläuterungen unter dem Text.)

Fontanestr. 34
04324 Leipzig
Germany(1)
14 July 2011

Dear John(,) (2)
Thanks for your last letter. I really had a good laugh when I read about your new English teacher and the way he tries to make you work harder for school. It's the same with my form teacher. If it was up to him, we would all stay indoors cramming for exams or preparing some sort of presentation. (3)
Anyway, it's only another four weeks to go until the summer break. Believe me, I need it. (4)
As you know, we won't be going anywhere this summer, so my mum and dad said that it would be perfectly fine for you to come and visit us.
We could do lots of things, and Leipzig is quite an interesting place, with lots of sights to visit and beautiful lakes where you can go for a swim or just chill out. And in the evenings, there are lots of parties going on. So the two of us could have a good time. Like we had in London last year. (5)
What do you think? Can you make it to Germany this year?
My family and I would be very pleased if you came to visit us this summer.
Look forward to hearing from you soon. (6)
Give my love to your mum and dad, and to Vivian of course. (7)

Yours (8)
Bernhard

(1) Wenn ihr euch gut kennt, muss die Adresse nicht mehr erwähnt werden. (Sie kann aber immer stehen.)

(2) Andere Möglichkeiten: Hello/Hi/...
Das Komma kann weggelassen werden.
(3) Man sollte auf den vorigen Brief eingehen und auf den Inhalt (hier: der neue Englischlehrer) reagieren, also mit seinem Partner kommunizieren.
(4) Überleitung zum eigentlichen Anliegen (Einladung).
(5) Das Miteinander bzw. die Gegenseitigkeit der Beziehung wird betont.
(6) Du bittest um Antwort. Andere Formulierungen wären: Write back soon, Hope to hear from you, I'm looking forward to hearing from you.
(7) Hier könnte auch stehen: Give my regards to, regards to (Diese Formulierungen sind etwas „neutraler", also angebracht, wenn man jemanden noch nicht so gut kennt.)
(8) Andere Grußformeln: See you (CU), Love, Lots of love, wenn ihr euch sehr gut kennt. (Love und Lots of love wird eher von Mädchen/Frauen verwendet.)
Ansonsten geht: All the best, Take care, Best wishes

Exercise 2 Seite 80

1. False. In a personal letter you may use informal language.
2. False. Formal letters start with "Dear Sir or Madam" if you do not know the person's name. Otherwise address them by their name: Mr/Mrs/Ms Jacobs
3. True
4. False. Name and address of the receiver are put on the left below the address of the sender.
5. True
6. False. They do mind.
7. False. You should not use contractions in formal letters.
8. True
9. False. Only if you don't know people's names.
10. True

Exercise 3 Seite 81

Lösungsvorschlag mit Erläuterungen (Die Ziffern im Brief verweisen auf die Erläuterungen unter dem Text.)

Prager Straße 123
65545 Bad Camberg
Germany
14 March 2012

Language Holidays UK
33 Teasel Way
London E15 9RT

Dear Sir or Madam,
I am interested in the language courses advertised in the latest edition of "English International", and I would be very grateful if you could send me further information about the programmes you offer and about prices. (1)
Could you please tell me how many lessons a week are offered and how many people there are in one class?
As I am very fond of sports, I would also like to know if the language course could be combined with some sporting activities. I am particularly interested in surfing and rugby.
My English is good enough to communicate more or less fluently, but I do have a problem with writing essays. Do you offer any special writing classes?
I look forward to hearing from you.

Yours faithfully, (2)
Michael Stahl (3)

(1) Trage dein Anliegen vor und beziehe dich auf die Informationsquelle.
(2) Wenn du den Namen des Ansprechpartners nicht kennst, dann steht „Yours faithfully". Wenn der Ansprechpartner namentlich bekannt ist, scheibt man „Yours sincerely". (Im amerikanischen Englisch geht auch Sincerely, Sincerely Yours oder Yours Truly)
(3) Unter deiner (lesbaren) Unterschrift steht noch einmal dein gedruckter Name.

Exercise 4 Seite 82

Dear Jake,
What a nice idea to meet at your local rabbit club exhibition. Thank you for the invitation. But I'm afraid public transport doesn't provide proper services on Saturdays. Anyway, instead of looking at different rabbits - which I'm not too keen on - I'd really much rather meet you in Washington where we could visit the newly opened Sea Life exhibition and later on watch the movie "Shark V".
I hope you'll also find my suggestion interesting.
Looking forward to hearing from you.
CU

Markus

4.2 Statistiken/Umfragen beschreiben

Exercise 1 Seite 83

1. These statistics say that there is a sharp increase in the rate of criminal offences.
2. The number of unemployed people has decreased.
3. From these statistics we can conclude that the problem hasn't been solved yet.
4. There is/are not enough data to support this assumption.
5. The majority of people can't survive without their car.

Exercise 2 Seite 83

1. statistics, 2. survey, 3. increase,
4. decrease, 5. majority, 6. minority

4.3 Die allgemeine Bildbeschreibung

Exercise 1 Seite 84

Lösungsvorschlag:

There is a big circle. Inside the circle at the top there's a small square. On the right at the side there are two small triangles. On the left there's a cross and there are two dots at the bottom. In the middle there is a small rectangle.

Exercise 2 Seite 85

1. This has a frightening effect on the observer.
2. The artist has chosen these colours in order to make the picture even more impressive.
3. This symbol might stand for the United Kingdom.
4. The expression on his face, as well as his body language, shows that he is very angry.
5. The old castle in the top half of the picture might represent the King's power.
6. The heart is used to symbolize love.
7. In this picture by da Vinci you can see an unknown woman.

4.4 Cartoons beschreiben

Exercise 1 Seite 86

1. In this picture Great Britain is shown as a lion.
2. The lion symbolizes power and determination.
3. The cartoon expresses that Great Britain didn't treat its colonies fairly.
4. The whole depiction is, of course, quite exaggerated.
5. The caption (statement below the picture) is not supposed to be taken literally.
6. This shows that the situation of immigrants is very difficult.

Exercise 2 Seite 86

Lösungsvorschlag:

In the left-hand corner of the cartoon there is a fish-like animal coming out of the water. The animal thinks "Eat, survive, reproduce". To the right of that animal there is another animal that looks like a lizard. It also thinks "Eat, survive, reproduce". Next to the lizard there is an animal that resembles a small dragon. It also thinks "Eat, survive, reproduce". Right next to the dragon-like animal there is an animal that looks like a monkey. It thinks "Eat, survive, reproduce" as well. Next to the monkey there is a man. He has got his hands in his trouser pockets, looks straight ahead and thinks "What's it all about?"
After having studied the cartoon in detail, I think it is about evolution and the difference between animals and human beings. Millions and millions of years ago, the first animals lived in the water. One day, they came out of the water and slowly developed into different animals and finally into human beings. However, animals live by instinct and only "think" about food, survival and reproduction. Human beings are different, as is shown in the

cartoon. They don't live by instinct alone, they think that there has to be something else. That's why the man in the cartoon wants to know what it (= life) is all about. He is searching for a deeper meaning, for a purpose. I think the author of the cartoon wants to make fun of our need for meaning. For millions of years of evolution, eating, surviving and reproducing were the most important things - so maybe they are what it's all about and there really is no deeper meaning.

4.5 Personen beschreiben

Exercise 1 Seite 89

1. Ich mag ihn eigentlich nicht. Er ist einfach zu ehrgeizig und egoistisch/selbstsüchtig. Kein Wunder, dass er der unbeliebteste Junge in der Klasse ist.
2. In der Geschichte wird die Frau als eher schüchtern und zurückgezogen dargestellt. Vielleicht liegt es daran, dass sie nicht selbstbewusst genug ist, um den ersten Schritt zu tun.
3. Dieser Junge verhält sich so kindisch. Er ist nicht vernünftig genug, einen Helm aufzusetzen. Eines Tages wird er im Rollstuhl enden.
4. Sein Verhalten gegenüber seinem Vater war wirklich schändlich. Ich denke, er sollte mehr Respekt zeigen und sensibler/einfühlsamer sein.
5. Als sie den Wettbewerb gewannen, gaben sie überhaupt nicht damit an. Im Gegenteil, sie waren sehr bescheiden.

Exercise 2 Seite 90

1. She seems to be a sensible child.
2. You should be proud of your son.
3. John has been jealous of James for years.
4. I consider him to be a rather unpleasant character/person.
5. Sue thinks he is a little too ambitious.
6. You should relax a little.
7. You are really taking everything too seriously.
8. Try to be more self-confident.
9. He had never seen such an insecure/self-conscious person.
10. He turned out to be a very pleasant person.

Exercise 3 Seite 90

1. proud of, 2. ambitious, 3. insecure/self-conscious/indecisive, 4. selfish, 5. shy

Exercise 4 Seite 90

1. lazy, 2. skilful/dexterous, 3. self-conscious, 4. foolish, 5. inconsiderate, 6. outgoing, 7. harmless, 8. unpleasant, 9. easy-going, 10. insensitive, 11. irresponsible, 12. immature, 13. unsociable, 14. indecisive

Exercise 5 Seite 91

Lösungsvorschlag:
The man in the photograph is about 30 years old and has an angry look on his oval face. His brown hair is very short and straight, and his ears are small. He is frowning and there is sweat on his forehead. There is a deep line between his dark, thick eyebrows. He is staring at something so that his green eyes look cross-eyed. His nose is straight with wide nostrils. He has opened his thin-lipped mouth widely and seems to be shouting something. His teeth are in good condition, but while his upper front teeth are very even, his lower front teeth are askew (= not straight). He is clean-shaven and his neck is strong. He is wearing a white and red sports shirt.

4.6 Textarbeit/Textanalyse

Exercise 1 Seite 94

1. convey/express the idea, 2. is set in, 3. events, 4. emphasizes, 5. concludes

Exercise 2 Seite 94

1. A novel by George Orwell.
2. In the text it says ...
3. The story is set in ...
4. The author says that ...
5. ... taken from a newspaper

4.7 Stellung beziehen

Exercise 1 Seite 95

1. I strongly disagree./I don't agree at all.
2. You are right there.
3. In my opinion, there are no arguments to support that.
4. Statistics show that the situation has improved.
5. I don't think that makes sense.

Exercise 2 Seite 95

1. has improved, 2. are certain/are convinced, 3. I (strongly) disagree, 4. evidence shows, 5. am convinced

4.8 Sprachmittlung/Mediation

Exercise 1 Seite 96

Lösungsvorschlag:

The article is about a campaign to support street children. It was carried out by class 6c from our school in cooperation with "Terre des Hommes". The children went to the town centre and acted like street children. Some of the people passing by were friendly and helpful, others reacted in a rather hostile way. The whole event was covered by the media and the children were given a special award by a German TV station.

4.9 Übersetzung

Exercise 1 Seite 98

1. tatsächlich - gegenwärtig
2. werden - bekommen
3. jemandem die Schuld geben - jemanden bloßstellen
4. die Wüste - der Nachtisch
5. mutig - brav
6. der Kritiker - die Kritik
7. berühmt - famos
8. die Kuppel - der Dom
9. freundlich - genial
10. das Geschenk - das Gift
11. hart - kaum (das Adverb von *hard* ist ebenfalls *hard*)
12. der Roman - der Römer
13. der Plan, die Landkarte - die Aktenmappe
14. der Boden, die Etage - der Flur
15. der Mord - der Mörder
16. die Notiz - die (Schul)Note
17. der Arzt - der Physiker
18. schwanger - prägnant
19. das Konservierungsmittel - das Präservativ
20. die Miete - die Rente
21. vernünftig - einfühlsam
22. der Bestatter, der Totengräber - der Unternehmer

Exercise 2 Seite 98

1. Sie wollte schon immer Bestatterin werden.
2. Das eigentliche Problem ist, dass ...
3. Sie geben viel Geld für wohltätige Zwecke aus.
4. Er gab mir ein Geschenk.
5. Das war eine interessante Vorlesung.
6. Es war ein seltsames Gewebe.
7. Wir sahen uns die Kuppel an.
8. Hast du den Kritiker gehört?
9. Du siehst müde aus. Ruhe dich aus.
10. Er hat has Gespräch belauscht.
11. Er bekam eine gute Miete.
12. Wo sind die Konservierungsmittel?
13. Dieser Junge beschuldigte mich vor der ganzen Klasse.

Exercise 3 Seite 99

1. Sie versuchten immer wieder, ein Tor zu schießen, doch leider vergebens.
2. Ich traf neulich einen guten Freund von ihm.
3. Was ihn betrifft, hatte er eine schwierige Zeit in New York.
4. Entschuldigung, aber du musst deine Rolle auswendig lernen.
5. Übrigens, er kam ziemlich spät nach Hause.

Exercise 4 Seite 100

1. Mein Vater geht morgens gern angeln.
2. Zufällig ist dieser Junge mein Bruder, also lass ihn in Ruhe.
3. Sie wanderte sehr gern in den Rocky Mountains.
4. Sie ist eine wunderbare Tänzerin. Sie wird wahrscheinlich eine große Karriere in London machen.
5. Früher habe ich immer in den teuersten Geschäften eingekauft.

Exercise 5 Seite 101

1. Sie waren die Ersten, die neue Pässe erhielten.
2. Beide wussten nicht, was sie tun sollten.
3. Weißt du, wie man dieses Problem lösen kann?
4. Als sie sahen, wer er war, begannen sie, mit ihren Hüten zu winken.
5. Es macht ihnen nichts aus, den Film noch einmal zu sehen.
6. Bitte entschuldigt mein Zuspätkommen, aber ich steckte in einem Verkehrsstau.

Test

Exercise 1 Seite 102

1.data, 2. statistics, 3.survey, 4. majority, 5. minority

Exercise 2 Seite 102

1. artists. → artistes/acrobats
2. on the picture. → in the picture
3. affect → effect
4. On the bottom → At the bottom
5. a wonderful picture from Titian. → a picture by Titian

Exercise 3 Seite 102

1. modest, 2. easy-going/relaxed, 3. self-confident, 4. mature, 5. shy/withdrawn

Exercise 4 Seite 103

1. selfish/egoistic, 2. ambitious, 3. self-confidence, 4. clumsy, 5. current/topical

Exercise 5 Seite 103

1. Es war ein tödliches Geschenk.
2. Er wurde ein berühmter Arzt.
3. Sie ist schwanger.
4. Wie hoch ist deine Miete?
5. Was für ein dummer Kritiker.

Exercise 6 Seite 103

1. They always donated a lot of money.
2. She became a successful entrepreneur/businesswoman.
3. Come on, be a good boy.
4. Have they got the murderer?
5. They/You are not really very sensitive.

Bibliographisches Institut GmbH, Dudenstraße 6, 68167 Mannheim
ISBN 978-3-411-87080-6

4 Read the definitions and write down the correct word.

1. You only think of yourself and don't care for others: You are ______.
2. People who work very hard to succeed are ______.
3. If you believe in yourself you have got some ______.
4. People who always fall over things are ______.
5. A problem that everyone is talking about right now is a ______ problem.

You get 1 point for each correct answer. Your points: ___ /5

5 False friends. Translate the following sentences into German.

1. It was a deadly gift.
2. He became a famous physician.
3. She is pregnant.
4. How much is your rent?
5. What a stupid critic.

You get 1 point for each correct answer Your points: ___ /5

6 False friends. Translate the following sentences into English.

1. Sie spendeten immer viel Geld.
2. Sie wurde eine erfolgreiche Unternehmerin.
3. Komm schon, sei ein braver Junge.
4. Haben sie den Mörder?
5. Sie sind wirklich nicht sehr sensibel.

You get 2 points for each correct answer. Your points: ___ /10

Your total points out of 35 points: ___

- More than 29? Very good.
- More than 26? Good.
- Less than 17? Have a look at the pages in this chapter again. You CAN do better.